Embracing Solitude

Embracing Solitude

Women and
New Monasticism

Bernadette Flanagan

with a contribution by Beverly Lanzetta
and a foreword by Rev. Dr. June Boyce-Tillman, MBE

CASCADE *Books* · Eugene, Oregon

EMBRACING SOLITUDE
Women and New Monasticism

Cascade Books
An Imprint of Wipf and Stock Publishers
199 W. 8th Ave., Suite 3
Eugene, OR 97401

www.wipfandstock.com

ISBN 13: 978-1-60608-337-6

Cataloging-in-Publication data:

Flanagan, Bernadette.

　　Embracing solitude : women and new monasticism / Bernadette Flanagan ; with a contribution by Beverly Lanzetta ; foreword by Rev. Dr. June Boyce-Tillman, MBE.

　　xxvi + 154 p. ; 23 cm—Includes bibliographical references and index.

　　ISBN 13: 978-1-60608-337-6

　　1. Monastic and religious life of women. 2. Solitude—Religious aspects—Christianity. 3. Spiritual life—Christianity. I. Lanzetta, Beverly. II. Tillman, June. III. Title.

BV4509.5 F52 2014

Manufactured in the USA

Scripture quotations come from the New Revised Standard Version Bile: Catholic Edition, copyright 1989, 1993, Division of Christian Education of the National Council of Churches of Christ in the United States of America. Used by permission. All rights reserved.

"Lost," by Ian Adams, is reprinted from Adams's 2010 book, *Cave, Refectory, Road: Monastic Rhythms for Contemporary Living*, with permission from the publisher, Canterbury Press, an imprint of Hymns Ancient and Modern.

In memory of

Sr. Columba Regan PBVM
d. 20 November 2009

A woman who loved to embrace the new movements of the Spirit

"All one need do is go into solitude and look upon God within oneself."
—TERESA OF AVILA,
The Way of Perfection 28:2

Contents

Foreword

Rev. Dr. June Boyce-Tillman, MBE

Professor of Applied Music, University of Winchester

SOMETIMES A BOOK DROPS into your life at just the right time; and so it was for me when I received a draft of *Embracing Solitude*. I suspect it will be same for many others who in the light of the current developments in Christian spirituality share my hopes. I have read a great deal of this book in Winchester Cathedral during performances and rehearsals of *Chronicles of Light*. It was as if the ancient monastic voices came alive in a new and exciting way on these pages, and were in tune with today's music.

At the same time as reading the draft of *Embracing Solitude* I received a novel by the founder of Sacred Life-Arts,[1] Dana Reynolds—*Ink and Honey*—which explores a similar vision through the medium of a novel that documents a fictional new sisterhood of visionaries, healers, and mystics: the Sisters of Belle Coeur. The exploration of the same theme in two different forms indicates how much it is the spirit of our age. Indeed a third event, when I was given the poem below about Queen Boadicea, who inspired and led the largest revolt against Roman rule in Britain, also seemed to summarize the themes of courageous, heart-based women's leadership in this book well:

> I am the Voice dispossessed of the tangible,
> The truth that sees the whole of history outstretched;
> I tell of past events long since put out of mind,
> Of woes, tribulations, ingratitude and guile,
> Of strength and valour in the face of oppression,
> Of wickedness that repeats through history,

---

1. Online: http://sacredlifearts.com

For people change not, thus the events that they fashion
Reflect inevitably things past. So beware!
Be on guard! Perils wait! Be vigilant and watch!
All those that have ears to hear, learn and understand
That covert webs of power shackle a hapless world,
Spun by Mammon's avaricious, ruthless, hard spawn,
The men of mendacity, the engineers of fate:
A wise sage said: "O Death, where is thy victory?"
Boudica's reply: "There is no death for the brave."[2]

For all intentional spiritual seekers this is a vital text, for it provides a myriad of insights to enrich their practice with helpful questions at the end of each of the introductory inspirational chapter. The increasingly common usage of the nomenclature *spiritual seeker* for people who wish to challenge the worst effects of an increasingly secularized marketplace has, however, resulted in a number of losses. Not the least of these is a sense of community belonging. Carrette and King have pointed out that individuality in the models of spiritual seeking is so rooted in the archetype of the essentially solitary heroic journey that it effectively defends contemporary society against corporate assaults on its injustices, such as those mounted by the Church in former times against such violences as slavery.[3] This book sets out a variety of ways that this sense of community may be retrieved. It critiques many of the givens of our culture—the centrality of work to our identity, the discrediting of a vow of chastity, and the centrality of the natural family to the fabric of society.

Spiritual Seeking

Much of today's faith seeks understanding and transformation through a widening out of the search to a variety of spiritual traditions, here explored through the development of the Interfaith Seminary in the final chapter. This approach to faith longs for a personal holiness and desires to creatively make new contemporary rituals of belonging and trusting, a subject about which several texts have been published in the last twenty years.[4] This book links spiritual seeking effectively with the history of

2. Shute, *Boudica the Great*, 1.

3. Carrette and King, *Selling Spirituality*.

4. Bell, *Ritual Theory, Ritual Practice*; Apffel-Marglin, *Subversive Spiritualities*; Drane, *Spirituality to Go*.

spirituality through the rediscovery of the diverse forms of the feminine quest for God. The insight of feminist theologians about the "becoming" nature of God, the presence of Sophia at the heart of everyday living, and the deep desire within humanity to journey into God and incarnate the Divine is the weft of the woven tapestry of contemporary spiritual seeking: all are subliminally in evidence in the text.

Community

This book, written by a member of a religious community, suggests how structured, trustworthy spiritual companioning can be reestablished in new ways in contemporary secular society. I first met this idea when Mother Mary Clare of the Sisters of the Love of God[5] wrote the short easy-to-read book *The Contemplative in the World.*[6] At last one did not need to withdraw to lead the contemplative life! This was a huge relief for a young, spiritually aware girl like myself, who felt called to a contemplative life, but who also had the obligation, as an only child, to bear the grandchildren. I developed, as suggested here, an inner monastery, which has always served me well, even when more recently technology has threatened to invade the quality of solitude.

The spiritual life has always set up a variety of complex, mixed images for women (more so than for men), as the vocation to family life has not been laid so heavily by the church on men as on women. Leaders of women's religious orders such as Mother Emily of the Sisters of the Church,[7] when they were reestablished within Anglicanism, were critiqued for drawing women away from their main calling of bearing children and caring for a family. But here we have the stories of women from history who have had both a spiritual life and a married life, and of contemporary women who are also finding ways of combining the two.

This book makes three significant contributions:

- A creative engagement with the increasing decline in church attendance

- New ways of pursuing a spiritual search within the context of a dispersed community

5. Online: http://www.slg.org.uk/.

6. Mary Clare, *The Contemplative in the World.*

7. Online: http://www.sistersofthechurch.org/.

- A history of the monastic archetype from a feminine perspective, which has, in general, been missing from mainstream church history

Women

At the heart of the suppression of the feminine by the churches is the fact that stories of women have been neglected, systematically deleted, ridiculed, and ignored. In *Embracing Solitude* women's involvement in works of charity and spiritual education is, by contrast, celebrated and honored. I loved, in particular, the rediscovery of transformative weeping, evident also in the life of Margery Kempe, as an established part of women's spirituality—an effective antidote to its portrayal by the much later school of psychiatric medicine as hysteria. The gendered dimensions of concepts such as rules of life and pilgrimage are exposed through the histories of religious women presented here.

Women's Communities

Developments within communities of women are historicized and contemporized—the availability and vulnerability of women throughout history whose lives have been consumed by a passion for the infinite—developments that have seldom formed part of the grand narrative of the churches. The marriage between solitude and community runs through the entire text like a leitmotif, as the life and rules of hermits and anchoresses are noted and compared with people choosing to live out a life of contemplation in the world of the everyday and to discover the mystery within the complexity of contemporary life. However, the theme of solitude not as a failure to find a partner but as an inner resource is an exciting one for those of us who have chosen to live our lives this way as a conscious choice, rather than as an enforced necessity. This runs counter to most contemporary advertising, which now sees partnership (both heterosexual and homosexual) as essential to full humanity. Silence, solitude, simplicity, solidarity, prayer, and the dilemmas of obedience run as recurring tropes throughout the text. I delighted in the idea of developing a connected solitude; a number of spiritual practices to enable it are set out in *Embracing Solitude*. The idea of belonging without boundaries is an effective antidote to the narrow perspective of the contemporary emphasis on the enclosed nuclear family with its narrow intimacy and its potentially sordid secrets.

The need for companionship in the midst of the journey into solitude is differently expressed in a variety of stories, and many contemporary expressions are helpfully explored. Indeed as a survey of contemporary monasticism alone, *Embracing Solitude* is outstanding. I now see developing around me the idea of soulful conversation in a companionship of friends, which for me started first in the groups of women meeting for worship in hidden and private groups in the 1970s.

Intuition

The solitude movements of contemporary spirituality—a rising tide in many different parts of the world today—is often, to use the Foucauldian terms which I explore in *Unconventional Wisdom*,[8] an attempt to recover ways of knowing subjugated in contemporary Enlightenment-governed society. A critical way of knowing in these uncertain times is intuition, given especially its role in religious experience. This is very carefully explored as a recurring theme in this book, particularly in the history of women religious from various ages and traditions. The fragility of spiritual awareness and its vulnerability to patriarchal oppression is beautifully described.

I particularly liked the linking of Evelyn Underhill's work on mysticism—phases of awakening, enacting and simplifying, illumination of purpose, and impasses and suffering (a pain often too deep for words)—to the autobiographies of women. This provides an extremely helpful and insightful overview of these narratives, which have been proliferating over the last twenty years. The development of mystical solitude as a type of imaginal space, particularly as related to Nano Nagle's ultimate establishment of the Presentation Sisters, I found very informative; as I did also the notion of a mystagogic reading of texts—which opens up new ways of academic research.

If some of the spiritual seeking of the last fifty years has portrayed mystical experience as something like a finding celestial Smarties, candies scattered from heaven to make people's lives better, spiritualities based in a notion of nonattachment to the world and deaf to the cries of the suffering are heavily critiqued through the lens of the stories of women

8. Boyce-Tillman, *Unconventional Wisdom*.

of the past and the present in this collection. This book throughout its course seeks to reinforce both in the past and today the link between transformative inner solitude and innovative social action, providing ample illustration of the position of Dorothee Soelle in her seminal text, *The Silent Cry*.[9]

The monastic archetype is set out in a myriad of different forms in history which are interrogated and critiqued as a way of finding new expressions for it, in a world where the creation of vibrant spiritual communities is a deep challenge on a number of fronts.

The Arts

As a composer and performer, I find it wonderful to meet others exploring the place of the arts in emerging spiritual movements such as the new monasticism. There was a loss in women's music-making when the great religious houses were dispersed, since these communities were centers where figures like Hildegard of Bingen (1098–1179) and Chiara Margarita Cozzolani (1602—ca. 1676–1678) had found their creativity; the notion that the arts as media for spiritual exploration is being rediscovered with the Internet's Abbey of the Arts offers exciting new possibilities for artistic spiritual creativity. The metaphor of the dance is used for the development of these new impulses, and there is helpful debate about the embodied nature of women's spirituality and where asceticism might fit in women's narratives—whether as spiritual practice or as part of Weight Watchers. The expression of women's spirituality as intimate relationship with Christ explored in visions and expressed in writing and song is an ongoing possibility that is little explored in contemporary literature.

This book speaks to the deepest longings of spiritual seekers today. It answers many of their questions, places them in an historical context, and most of all encourages them on their pilgrimage into the heart of God through a mysticism embodied in a shared spiritual solitude that can be maintained in the midst of the ordinary and the everyday. Just as Christian seekers moved from the city to the desert in the third century, now the move is back to finding contemplative solitude in the midst of the commerce of the city.

9. Soelle, *The Silent Cry*.

Preface

SIMPLE EVENTS CAN REVEAL to us how rapidly our world is changing. I write this preface in the middle of the most severe occurrence of snow and ice ever experienced in Ireland. News bulletins have become the lighthouses providing guidance through the ever-changing landscape. However, these news bulletins presume that the average person seeking to make his or her way to any of the major ports of life—work, family, doctor, church, or shops—has the technology available to access the information being provided to the public so as to get out and about safely. Tweeting, texting, and web-browsing are the vernacular of this emergency situation. We are asked not to travel to the airport until we first check the website of our air carrier, and the bus company tweets its latest updates. A change of consciousness is dawning. We have crossed a digital rubicon and to choose to opt out of digital communication is becoming equivalent to choosing to live without electricity.

In a similar manner, we have crossed a spiritual rubicon in Western society, one that has had a particularly intense expression in Ireland. Wave after wave of revelation of clergy misconduct, of the abuse of children in religious-run institutions, of the disregard for society's laws by religious leaders, and of the gross mistreatment of adult women in Magdalene laundries has stripped away the comfort of former spiritual blankets. As a nation Ireland has come to the threshold of a new spiritual consciousness, an event that in other parts of the world may be more locally or individually circumscribed. In traversing this unknown place Ireland has unique resources to call on because of its spiritual history.

In this book I intend to reflect on the themes, trends, and metaphors that underpin a discussion of solitude as a creative response to the unknown, and to outline practical expressions of the contemporary turn. I also aim to present the unexplored resources of guidance and support in these challenging times available through the lives and writings of those who embraced the monastic enterprise across the ages as a journey into personal authenticity. I focus on women because forgotten, neglected legacies may have a freshness that overused resources may lack at this time. In a similar vein, the abbot of the Benedictine community in Glenstal Abbey in County Limerick has suggested that it is artists who may lighten the way in the undrawn spiritual landscape that now presents itself. In his evocatively titled book *Underground Cathedrals*,[1] Abbot Mark Patrick Hederman, OSB, has sketched how the imaginative legacy of prominent figures in the Irish arts world, such as Brian Friel, Louis le Brocquy, and Seamus Heaney present subtle hints of the spiritual sensibility of our times. I turn to monastic voices old and new to light a lantern for traversing the dark alleyways of the Spirit in which we now find ourselves: Moninne, from the Celtic tradition, and her companions in Spirit; Syncletica, from the early Egyptian-desert spiritual initiative; Marie d'Oignies, who pioneered lay spirituality eight hundred years ago in Belgium; Angela Merici, who created innovative spiritual community in Italy; and Nano Nagle, who forged a pathway of the Spirit in the context of unfavorable sociopolitical circumstances in eighteenth-century Ireland. I finally turn to contemporary women who are embracing solitude in new ways today and again allowing its fruits to enrich the land of the Spirit in our midst. One innovator, Beverly Lanzetta, has provided a personal account of the contours of her journey, a contribution for which I am very grateful.

1. Hederman, *Underground Cathedrals*.

Acknowledgments

IT IS A PRIVILEGE to thank all those who made this book possible. This publication reflects conversations with many women who have shared with me their sense of living at the end of one season of spiritual time and at the beginning of another season of time. I thank Ian Adams, Bernie Baker, Kathleen Barrett, Iva Beranek, Margaret Benefiel, Carmel Boyle, Mary Brennan, Elaine Burke, James Clarke, Cyprian Consiglio, Sandra Curran, Amanda Dillon, Isoilde Dillon, Anne Marie Dixon, Anthony Grimely, Kieran Hayes, Geraldine Holton, Suzanne Kelly, Jean Kilcullen, Michael Hayes, Margaret Mulcaire, Michael Murray, Joan O'Hare, Briege O'Hare, Helen O'Keeffe, Mary Quinn, Barbara Raftery, Veronica Ryan, Joshua Searle, Ray Simpson, and Phyllis Zagano.

I owe much to an attentive listening presence in the person of Gertrude Howley, who has shared my journey through its changing seasons since 1976 and has provided an abundance of encouragement, perspective, humor, and hospitality throughout this writing project. When providing all this generous support, she has often included me a wider circle of kindness provided by Chris Mulcahy and the community of Presentation Sisters at Youghal Road, Dungarvan, Co Waterford. For all the warm hospitality provided I am truly grateful. Bernadette Purcell, Una Trant, and Kathleen Meagher, who have been my dispersed community of Presentation companions during the writing of this book acted as midwives to its safe delivery. Sr. Claude Meagher, Provincial leader for the South East Province of Presentation Sisters, provided practical resources to start this project by supporting participation in the MONOS gatherings in the United Kingdom.

Many scholars shared their time and expertise in advising on various historical details in the text: Dr. Elva Johnson, Dr. Cynthia Bourgeault, Dr. Johnathan Wooding, Prof. Douglas Burton Christie, Dr. Beverly Lanzetta, and Dr. Peter Tyler. The support of the librarians at Milltown

Institute—Mary Glennon, Anne O'Carroll, Mary Perrem (RIP), and Áine Stack—was invaluable in retrieving from the Irish library collection items that otherwise would have been very difficult to access. Helen Bradley, Librarian at All Hallows College, has generously facilitated interlibrary access.

Finally, I acknowledge my debt of gratitude to my colleague Michael O'Sullivan, SJ. He has witnessed the various incarnations of several sections of this text. As a companion in the work of clearing a path for the study of spirituality in the university, he has regularly drawn my attention to emerging publications and conferences that complemented the themes of the book. For this and the many hours spent on detailed commentary and feedback on the text I am enormously grateful.

Introduction

THE NUMBERS OF WOMEN living singly in Western societies is on the increase, and a very insightful transnational study that explores the varying expressions of this phenomenon is provided in Eric Klinenberg's *Going Solo*.[1] He highlights how in the publications of the individual writers who have explored the phenomenon, it is evident that their interpretations are often borrowed from history and literature. Consequently the loneliness and eccentricity, sometimes associated with spinsterhood in such sources, can overshadow the personal narratives of women living singly. Alternatively, the contemporary single woman (and man) may be presented as an icon of major social trends such as individualism and the breakdown of social bonds—another interpretation that the research of Klinenberg challenges strongly. In a similar vein Dr. Jan Macvarish, a sociologist from the University of Kent, England, has spent several years studying the lives of single women, has published her research findings,[2] and is a member of the Scholars of Single Women Network.[3] Her work shows that though the number of those living singly has grown significantly, the meaning of the statistical shift in the domestic arrangements of women is still not clear. It is evident from the biographies being produced among this population that discussions regarding women's life choices ought not reduce these choices solely to changed social opportunities. The fact that the women who are choosing this new single living arrangement are generally well-educated professionals presents all scholars, including those in religious studies, with the challenge of thoughtfully engaging with this phenomenon. *Embracing Solitude* is one such contribution.

In setting about this study, it is recognized that the resistance to accepting the phenomenon of women intentionally embracing solitude

1. Klinenberg, *Going Solo*.
2. Macvarish "What Is the 'Problem' of Singleness."
3. See http://www.medusanet.ca/singlewomen/index.htm/.

as a spiritual practice has a long history. In 1681 the French ecclesiastic Jean Bâptiste Thiers (1636–1703) remarked, "Une religieuse hors de sa clôture est . . . comme un arbre hors de terre; . . . comme un poisson hors de l'eau . . . comme une brebis hors sa bergerie et en danger d'être dévorée des loups."[4]

The concept for this book has had a long gestation and has emerged from not only the social-science data regarding the changing demographics of women's living arrangements but also the cultural expressions of the reevaluation of solitude. A particular instance of the latter that this author observed was the screening of the film *Into Great Silence*[5] in the Irish Film Institute in January 2007. The crowds far exceeded expectations, and so it was necessary to bring the film back for a second run—the only film in the 2007 listings to require a second screening. This 162-minute documentary created an experience for the viewer of the intense solitude of Carthusian life in the nine-hundred-year-old Grand Chartreuse monastery. A similarly unexpected positive reception of this award-winning documentary was experienced in Germany and Italy. The filmmaker, Philip Gröning, in an interview regarding the film, views it as not merely documentary but rather didactic: "the time when you can base your self-concept on work is over . . . and everyone is afraid of what will happen next . . . The function of a human being is not to work. The function of a human being is to be aware."[6]

In a similar vein, a theatrical exposition of the parallels between Hildegard of Bingen and contemporary women living in solitude in urban rented rooms and apartments received a warm reception in Dublin. Ian Wilson created this acoustic theatre project titled *Una Santa Oscura*. It was premiered in March 2010 and received four further performances at the October 2010 Dublin Theatre Festival. The evocative combination of

---

4. "A woman religious living outside of cloister is like a tree that is not rooted in the earth, or a fish that is out of water, or a sheep that is not in its sheepfold and is in danger of being devoured by wolves" (personal translation). See *Traité de la clôture des religieuses* (Dezallier, 1681). Original from Lyon Public Library (Bibliothèque jésuite des Fontaines).

5. A German filmmaker, Philip Gröning, applied in 1984 to the Grand Chartreuse in order to film the Carthusian way of life. Sixteen years later the community was ready to receive him as a guest for six months, during which time he made the film without the usual technical supports that filmmakers use. The film won a Special Jury Prize at the Sundance Festival in 2006.

6. See *Journal of Religion and Film* 10/1 (2006); http://www.unomaha.edu/jrf/vol10no1/sundance2006.htm/.

musical pieces performed by the acclaimed violinist Ioana Petcu-Colan and video visuals by Jack Phelan, which lit up the walls of the tiny living space with the images of urban developments such as cranes, created a tangible sense of the coincidence of opposites. Whatever the changes in the external landscape, there is a suggestion that women continue in the tradition of Hildegard of Bingen to attune to the music of the inner being from which life is entered with a more compassionate and peace-creating presence.

A changing sense of the meaning of embracing solitude has presented itself to me not only in cinema and theater but also in the classroom. For almost ten years, in the late nineties and into the new millennium, I taught a module titled Consecrated Life: Theology and Practice, in Milltown Institute, Dublin. Each year, the same sessions in the module seemed to have an engaging and enlivening effect on the participants. The sessions in question were the ones where the history of consecrated life was presented. An important text for this presentation was Philip Sheldrake's article, "Revising Historical Perspectives," which was published in an edition of *The Way Supplement* and explored the theme "Religious Life in Transition."[7] In this article Sheldrake challenged readers to "question the assumption, not only that the foundational model for religious life was cenobitic-monastic, but that its development moved in a single line."[8] He went on to outline the many expressions of the committed, singular quest for God that are regularly excluded from an account of the history of consecrated life. These expressions, particularly the Beguines, always generated imaginative engagement for participants in the module and most significantly among younger women students. It is in the spirit of thoughtful seeking for new manifestations of culturally sensitive expressions of the core identity of spiritually focused lives, which I experienced during these discussions, that I approach my current project.

New, rich interpretations of traditional practices associated with the God quest—poverty, celibacy, fasting, pilgrimage, solitude, social solidarity, asceticism—are reconfiguring the analysis of the core of lives of commitment to spiritual practice in discussions of the new monasticism. Under the influence of the French philosopher Michel Foucault, these practices no longer are considered primarily as moral behaviors but are viewed as modes of expression, through which individuals intentionally

7. Sheldrake, "Revising Historical Perspectives," 66–77.
8. Ibid., 68.

form personal identity. Foucault uses the term "technologies of the self" to refer to such practices and describes them as "those intentional voluntary actions by which men not only set themselves rules of conduct, but also seek to transform themselves, to change themselves in their singular being, and to make their life into an *oeuvre* that carries certain aesthetic values and meets certain stylistic criteria."[9]

Susanna Elm's reconsideration of the meaning of fourth-century ascetical practice among women in the deserts in Syria and Egypt has led the way in Foucauldian analysis of the classical accounts of the emergence of religious life in the deserts of Egypt and Syria.[10] In a similar manner, Belden Lane's extended reflection on the deep intersection between vocation and landscape in *The Solace of Fierce Landscapes*[11] has breached the boundaries of the classical, stable interpretations of the foundational structures of consecrated life, which tended to focus on withdrawal and protest. In particular, Lane has explored the paradox of landscapes that spiritual seekers inhabit and how harsh landscapes, such as mountain and desert, can heal. By implication, the suggestion exists in his work that solitary dwelling space can yield a profound spirituality of communion.

The particular way that I reflect on the trajectory of women embracing solitude across two millennia is informed by developments over the past quarter century in feminist biblical hermeneutics. Scholars such as Elisabeth Schüssler Fiorenza, Margot H. King and Sandra Schneiders have built up the theoretical (in terms of hermeneutics) and practical (in terms of translations of texts regarding womens' lives) frameworks that implicitly underpin the historical work in the chapters of this book where I begin to thread together texts regarding the lives of women who are, or were, spiritual innovators.[12] In each life, immersion in intentional solitude is/was fundamental to their spiritual contribution/legacy. Thus the horizon within which the texts of women's lives and writings (Syncletica, Moninne, Marie d'Oignies, Angela Merici, Nano Nagle) will be read allows us to engage with the world in front of the text wherein these women are precursors to the solitude movement being described by contemporary women spiritual writers in the penultimate chapter and in the testimony of Beverly Lanzetta with which the book concludes. The

9. Foucault, *The History of Sexuality*, 2:10–11.

10. Elm, *"Virgins of God"*.

11. Lane, *The Solace of Fierce Landscapes*.

12. See Schneiders, *The Revelatory Text*; and Schüssler Fiorenza, *Bread Not Stone*.

solitude that their lives illustrate is a solitude of the heart, a cultivated inner garden of tranquillity wherein the authentic source of being may be encountered even in the midst of the feverish activity of life unfolding in all its abundance.

The particular way that I reflect on the recent widespread emergence of the phenomenon of solitude in the lives and writings of women spiritual teachers is informed by Margaret Funk's approach to *lectio divina*.[13] In other words I have taken an approach to reading the journals and writings of contemporary women about solitude that has engaged logical intelligence, symbolic intelligence, incarnational intelligence, and spiritual intelligence.[14] Consequently, the reflections that are assembled are enriched not only by consideration of current scholarship regarding the themes presented, but also by reflective attentiveness to the symbols that are woven into the texts and to the drama of living the text in daily life. The final selection of themes developed and explicated is often born out of the conversations of spiritual guidance where the Spirit of the age in which we live descends into consciousness with all the unexpectedness of a Pentecost awakening.

The ultimate commitment that underpins the reading of the texts could be described as mystagogic. In mystagogic research the focus is not on the analytical categories and structures of the materials being studied. As Kees Waaijman has indicated in his groundbreaking handbook for the study of spirituality, the mystagogical approach to textual research is imbued with "the experience of mystery, the mystery that is God."[15] The strategies of mystagogic research bear a close resemblance to the practice of *lectio divina* described above. It is an apophatic approach to scholarship, where the hidden mystery of a text is savored and received; rather than a cataphatic engagement where the text is deconstructed so as to yield up its treasure. Martin Laird has aptly noted in this context that

> there is a tendency among scholars to reduce apophatic theology to literary strategies (including methodologies). While these literary aspects have been ably demonstrated to characterize the apophatic genre . . . this trend in scholarship overlooks the fact that the apophatic tradition also presumes to a way of life. It is a simple life that leads to the experience of silence, to "the

13. Funk, *Lectio Matters*.

14. Ibid., 3.

15. Waaijman, "Mystagogic Research," in *Spirituality*, 870.

experience of non-experience" and not merely to an apophatic
style of theological thinking and writing.[16]

The life texts chosen in this work are replete with mystery; they speak of
the awesome adventure of life on the sea of God. The reading strategies
employed seek to respect this mystery.

Within the vast family of qualitative research methods available
today, this work might be described as an "appreciative inquiry." This
type of research approach focuses on seeds of life within the field of inquiry. It would be possible to feel sad or despondent about the decline
of familiar structures of mutual support in the spiritual journey and to
focus on what went wrong, the causes of decline, and planning solutions.
However, David Cooperrider, one of the leading advocates of appreciative inquiry, has observed that this approach to reflecting on reality is less
concerned with the problems that need to be solved and more focused on
appreciating, valuing, envisioning, and dialoguing about the mystery that
is ready to be embraced.[17]

The choice of lives that I have made is meant to be suggestive rather
than comprehensive. Although the presentation of these lives will not
have the detailed analysis that studies of each one of them individually
could set forth, it is hoped that presenting them within the horizon of
fruitful solitude and the emerging expressions of spiritual consciousness
characteristic of new monasticism will allow patterns to emerge that
might not otherwise be observed.

As well as a teacher, I am also a researcher and supervisor of research. In these roles I have a commitment to feminist standpoint theory.
This theory holds the view that gender is an influential factor in practices
of inquiry. In the case of this book, it supports the view that because
women are living now, and have lived in the past, in arrangements that
were transformed by intentional solitude, they have unique access to insights regarding this choice. This is not to suggest that these voices are
the sole voices to be given attention when reviewing the question being considered here. Rather, it is being proposed that the reflections of
women who have lived, or now live, within a new spiritual consciousness
that derives from the practice of intentional solitude can enrich the living understanding of new monasticisms. This standpoint also recognizes
that no research is value neutral, and holds the belief that mechanisms

16. Laird, "The 'Open Country Whose Name is Prayer,'" 141.

17. Cooperrider and Whitney, *Appreciative Inquiry*.

such as the public reception of published work are available to block the effects of wishful thinking and dogmatism.[18]

Finally, I acknowledge that the women presented here in the historical section are distinguished not only by the quality of their own inner awareness and responsiveness but also by the public leadership roles they assumed. Although they carved out their memorable enactments of fruitful solitude long before the science of leadership had been developed, they manifest what now might be called visionary leadership. In general, visionary leaders have more self-awareness and a greater capacity for reflective attunement than many others, and they tend to lead from the inside out. It is also the case that visionary leaders have a unique capacity to be adept at imagining new possibilities, and to create frameworks to support such possibilities. In general, they have an ability to draw on resources "outside the box" of current experience. In the spirit of Martin Luther King Jr., they have a dream for which they are willing to invest everything so that what they have sensed in solitude may take shape and give life in the fullness of day. Indeed in leadership science today the capacity for solitude is perceived as a leadership metacompetence.[19]

18. Harding, *The Feminist Standpoint Theory Reader*.

19. Bourantas, Athens University, http://www.mbaexecutive.gr/vdata/File/bibliothiki/Arthra/Solitude.pdf/.

Reflection on Solitude

I felt in need of a great pilgrimage so I sat still
for three days and God came to me.[1]

KABIR

There is no need to run outside for better seeing . . . Rather abide at
the center of your being; For the more you leave it the less you learn.
Search your heart and see . . . The way to do is to be.[2]

LAO-TZU

IN A WORLD SUFFERING the devastating effects of global, non-thinking greed and the abuse of power, the need to live with authenticity is increasingly being recognized as a personal obligation that no group or organization can overwrite. Since the emergence of the first wave of feminist consciousness in the late nineteenth and early twentieth centuries, the issue of women taking responsibility for the integrity of their own lives has been the subject of much critical reflection. Elizabeth Cady Stanton, a North American foremother of women's contemporary changing spiritual consciousness boldly declared,

> No matter how much women prefer to lean, to be protected and supported, nor how much men desire to have them do so, they must make the voyage of life alone, and for safety in an emergency they must know something of the laws of navigation. To guide our own craft, we must be captain, pilot, engineer; with chart and compass to stand at the wheel; to match the wind and

1. Ladinsky, translator. *Love Poems from God*, 227.
2. Bynner, translator, *The Way of Life according to Lao Tzu*, 55.

1

waves and know when to take in the sail, and to read the signs
in the firmament over all. It matters not whether the solitary
voyager is man or woman.[3]

While Stanton's address had a strong political motivation, the liberation that she envisioned for women would impact the intellectual, domestic, social, and spiritual domains of women's lives. Today, perhaps more than any other time in history, there is a rising collective awareness among women of the importance of learning to be still, attuned to a new consciousness as subtle as the movement of the wind and waves referred to in Stanton's speech. The challenge is to learn the art of cultivating the solitude necessary to live in deep attentiveness.

The art of learning wisdom through solitude is often depicted in association with garden imagery in spiritual traditions. In the Christian Scriptures Jesus spent his last few hours of freedom in the garden of Gethsemane.[4] This garden is the place of encounter with God in and through its being a place where the authentic articulation of a profoundly deep inner personal struggle takes place. The word *Gethsemane* derives from a combination of Hebrew words meaning "oil press," thus echoing its close proximity to the Mount of Olives. For almost two and a half thousand years the two-mile long ridge of the Mount of Olives has served as a major burial ground for the city of Jerusalem, and so the garden of Gethsemane served as a place of connection with those who had passed through the door of death. In this garden space Jesus comes to embrace the final chapter of his own life in solitude of heart and generosity of spirit.

Through the use of garden imagery in the book of the Song of Solomon in the Hebrew Scriptures, the intimacy with self and spirit, that the practice of solitude nurtures, is conveyed evocatively and intensely. In this collection of poems a garden, from which the dark and dismal atmosphere of winter has evaporated, is adorned with the bright and colorful mantle of springtime. This life-generating space is a metaphor of the fruitful intimacy which may arise for those who have the courage to embrace the solitude of such a non-urbanized space. The abundance of life in this garden environment—doves, lotuses, vines, figs, pomegranates—invites exploration. However, the author of the Song of Solomon

3. "Solitude of Self," Address Delivered by Elizabeth Cady Stanton before the Committee of the Judiciary of the United States Congress on Monday, January 18, 1892 in *The Women's Journal, January 23, 1892.*

4. Luke 22:39–46; Matthew 26:36–46; Mark 14:32–42.

reminds readers that the land of the spirit within each person is often "a garden locked" or "a fountain sealed" (4:12). Yet, if the winds of the spirit are invited to blow through this garden space, its fruitfulness will comfort many. "Awake, O north wind, and come, O south wind! Blow upon my garden, that its fragrance may be wafted abroad." (4:16). It is the truth that emerges from dwelling in each one's secret garden space that will heal and bring comfort. "O you who dwell in the gardens, my companions are listening for your voice; let me hear it" (8:13).

While biblical authors had a preference for gardens as locations of solitary intensity, other writers, like the ancient Greeks, used the idea of a dedicated landscape—valley, tree grove, or the like—*temenos,* to refer to spaces that nurtured distinct spiritual qualities in people. A *temenos* was usually associated with the territory of a god, goddess, or other spirit that could positively affect human life. The quality of a *temenos* was not created by the visible beauty of the landscape but rather by the invisible potency of spirit that inhabited the setting. Such physical spaces provided public nurturing grounds for the soul. On another level, these territories externalized the inner need for boundaried space—solitude—in order to cross the threshold of consciousness into the realm of spirit. The association of gardens, holy wells, and sacred groves with solitude has often meant that the notion of solitude has geographical associations that primarily depict separateness and isolation.

Whereas geographical representations of solitude may be evocative, I wish to suggest that solitude may perhaps be more helpfully considered from a psychospiritual point of view, whereby its main reference is that place within each person that is the center of spiritual consciousness. Solitude is a quality of heart that at various times has been acknowledged, celebrated, and nurtured through Sacred Heart spirituality.[5] Living from the heart space, which the invitation to embrace solitude points to, consists primarily in opening to the embrace of divine love. To live in this love one will constantly be challenged to cast off the old confinements of heart and to open oneself to the infinite horizons of love. It is a space into which the disciples were invited in the biblical scene of feeding the five thousand. Their first response to seeing the rising hunger of the crowd was to request Jesus to "send them away" (Luke 9:12). He did not reply by offering to feed the crowd himself but rather invited them to find that

---

5. Sacred Heart spirituality has not been solely devotional as is evidence from its impact on Pierre Teilhard de Chardin. See Grumett, *Teilhard de Chardin,* 94–99.

space in each of their own hearts from which the crowd might be fed: "You give them something to eat" (Luke 9:13).

The disciples reached into that well of love and compassion within themselves, a disposition that had been observed, appropriated, and acquired in the company of Jesus. In taking up the invitation of Jesus to feed the crowds themselves, they were invited to become connected to their own hearts so as to be connected with God's quality of loving compassion for a tired and hungry crowd. In the unfolding story of the feeding of the five thousand, it becomes evident that Jesus's own connection with the loving compassion of God has its foundation in the practice of gratefulness: "then Jesus took the loaves, and when he had given thanks, he distributed them to those who were seated; so also the fish, so much as they wanted" (John 6:11). Solitude enables one to observe the subtle actions of God that might otherwise go unnoticed. Solitude nurtures gratefulness, the personal capacity to recognize, acknowledge and appreciate love at work in the world.[6]

Solitude is a quality of personhood that facilitates singularity of purpose, through coming to know one's unique name. This is not just a matter of finding an acceptable and satisfying blend of involvements in life. Instead, solitude is the space where it is possible to discover the very essence of one's own being, what is utterly original and uniquely woven into the fabric of one's being. I am not an *it* to myself or to God, a project to be managed, a performer of tasks. I am a being which the Spirit is seeking to animate from when I wake to when I sleep. There is unity and integration at the heart of life, a silent music that calls each one to dance in its rhythm. Embracing solitude is the intentional creation of a space where we suspend the external music that can so easily set the pace and rhythm of our daily motion and where instead we redirect our attention to the more fundamental score of the Spirit. Leonard Cohen has aptly described this solitary space as a "Tower," and his lyrics in the song, "Tower of Song," invite reflection on the importance of commitment to spending time in the tower, "tied" to its interior landscape, in order to encounter the divine, inalienable core of one's being in the eyes of God.

Whereas external calm can facilitate the emergence and growth of Spirit-led living, the quest for solitude and a desire to be solitary do not necessarily coincide. Solitude is more an attitude than an environment: a lived belief in the need for regular withdrawal to the inner room of each

---

6. Emmons, *Thanks!*, 5.

one's being. Time spent in that inner monastery of being allows what has become muddied and confused in daily living to settle and become clear. In the spirit of Cohen's song, God is calling each one from within, to come home to the unique desire that has been placed in each heart by God. We seek to learn the mystery of God's desiring in our hearts, the truth of our life and being. Only in solitude can the music to which one is called to dance be heard. It is not effort and striving that makes a person vocationally genuine. The soul's voluntary alignment to its inner whispered name is the most essential act of abandonment into the energy of God. The ear of the heart seeks attentively to hear the unique name by which the spirit of being is called forth from a shadowy existence of accepted confinement into the vibrancy of life in abundance.

We can accumulate projects and plans but fail to attend to the most pressing life project: to embrace our personal unique journey on the sea of God, a journey externalized by ancient Irish monks like Brendan of Clonfert (c. 484—c. 577). Setting aside one's best-made maps is the first step in sailing to the guidance of the Spirit. On the silent open sea of the Spirit one becomes more finely attuned to the multiple subtle modes of guidance that prevail in this unique terrain. The heart that embraces such solitude is opened to dimensions of reality previously unnoticed. When the flow of life is embraced by solitude, eyes become more adept at noticing the hints of Presence since all existence sails in the sea of divine upholding. While embracing solitude seems at first to exclude, now it is clear that this sea sustains those who swim and dive and sail and float. In the place of solitude, we see the face of God in all who live and love. We are awakened to the burning bush of presence in what previously had been perceived as simply the haphazard, random drama of unfolding events.

Solitude of heart also enables each one to become home for the homeless. Pope John Paul II in a collection of teachings that he gave between 1979 and 1984, and which have become known as his *Theology of the Body*,[7] sought to reflect on how the most profound depths of a human being's identity might be brought into relationships. In these teachings John Paul II locates the foundations of his response in an "original solitude". Drawing on the account of creation in Genesis 2:15–25, he notes that the original identity of the human being is as one who has a depth capacity to open to the Divine, to be in the presence of God as one would

7. Percy, *The Theology of the Body Made Simple*.

be with a friend. In the images of walking and talking in the garden in the quiet of the evening, a sense of the original call of humanity being that of coming home to one's own heart is portrayed. One learns that without coming home to oneself one cannot be prepared for meeting and embracing creation and other human beings.

In attentive solitude our small self gradually melts so that the great self may emerge. The infinite energy of Divine love shared with each of us teaches us that it is only falling into this love that will make use free. Self-forgetting is the currency of intimacy with God. In the embrace of Love, self-forgetting arises not from negative asceticism but rather from the desire to be flooded with God. Relinquishing egoic striving becomes a daily practice of letting go, so that the greater energy of Love can emerge. We can however often harbor poorly informed notions of emptiness. In genuine self-emptying we are being drawn into freedom. Letting go is not a single absolute action, but a progressive sequence. Solitude is that reservoir within us that desires to receive the abundance of Love so that what is purely our own striving may flow away. In embracing solitude we are humbled by the magnificence of the Love we are offered.

In such an experience of solitude of heart a resting place for the weary traveler in today's world will be formed. Love of God alone happens in and through every encounter.

A flow of tears often greets such an overwhelming gift of compassionate presence, and the anguish of the heart is eased. In solitude of heart we learn the great beneficence of God. The Jewish mystical writer, Abraham Joshua Heschel (1907–1972) has poetically described this process of unlearning and awakening in his books *Man Is Not Alone* and *God in Search of Man*.[8] The process involves moving from knowing God mostly as object, something to be worshiped or praised, to learning to know God as subject: "He [God] appears as One Who demands, as One Who acts. Whose intention is to give righteousness and peace rather than to receive homage or adoration, Whose desire is to bestow rather than to obtain."[9]

In Heschel's mysticism God is in search of each person. No one's journey is irrelevant to God. It is at the well of solitude that we can learn of our place in God's dream for the world. It is difficult to wean ourselves away from the demands of the cultural acceleration in which we live and

---

8. Heschel, *God in Search of Man*; Heschel, *Man Is Not Alone*.

9. Heschel, *The Prophets: Part II*, 485.

in which we self-violate in response to cultural pressures. The gift arising from embracing solitude is to learn that we have access to spiritual affirmation from within. Although culturally we become habituated to acquisition and production, the embrace of solitude enables us to fall from the grip of this frame of mind and to fall into the arms of God. Solitude is a practice of dwelling in God's benevolence.

Living in awareness of this benevolence has the power to profoundly change the world in which we live—for the better. The conviction that the Benedictine monk and ashram founder Bede Griffiths (1906–1993) shared regarding such possibilities is wrought from a lifetime of contemplative living. It represents the fruits of forty years of nurturing and sustaining the practices of external silence and inner attentiveness within which the stillness to hear the voice of the Spirit is cultivated.

> There can be no stillness without discipline, and the discipline of external silence can help us towards the inner tranquillity which is at the heart of authentic religious experience. In meditation we take steps to achieve this stillness. We quieten our bodies and our emotions, then, gradually allow the mind to become single-pointed. Stillness within one individual can affect society beyond measure.[10]

Bede Griffths biographer Shirley Du Boulay has highlighted his dream that such a contemplative stance would not be confined to enclosed monastics since the need in society for those who could hold such still spaces amidst conflict and turmoil is not diminishing.

> Unless human life is centered on the awareness of a transcendent reality which embraces all humanity and the whole universe, and at the same time transcends our present level of life and consciousness, there no hope for humanity as a whole . . . The aim of every community should be to enable its members to realize this transcendent mystery in their lives and communicate their experience to others.[11]

Robert Sardello's investigation of the nature of silence[12] is particularly powerful in its assertion that silence is a fundamental commitment to receive the transcendent mystery present in the encounters of life. For Sardello, silence is not a passive act of disassociation; instead it is the

---

10. Cited in Spink, *The Universal Christ: Daily Readings with Bede Griffiths*, 31.

11. Du Boulay, *Beyond the Darkness*, 247.

12. Sardello, *Silence*.

condition of receptivity. In invoking inner silence in any life situation a person opens to a meditative attentiveness to the true voice of the other, a stance of openness to mystery.

While Griffths's words provide encouragement and challenge to those undertaking a journey into solitude, they do not replace the task of drawing a new map for today's journey, a map that will speak to us of the challenges of living this wisdom, often without the support of monastic rhythms and ashram-taught discipline. There are distinctive new features in twenty-first-century literature that explores the art of how to quiet our bodies and emotions. The most notable of these new trends is that the quest to live life from within a practice of solitude and stillness is no longer exclusively confined to professional monastics. The forms in which the new discourse of solitude presents itself are many and varied, but the legacy of previous understandings always enrich the discussion.

Solitude has a wide circle of associated concepts. Stillness, silence, solitariness, aloneness, isolation, quiet, retreat, and privacy are some of the realities that get blended into the mixture when a discussion of solitude is taking place. Terms with more negative associations, such as *loners, isolation,* and *disengagement* can also sometimes appear. In his extensive reflection on solitude, Philip Koch[13] has provided a brilliant overview of the historical suspicion of solitude, even from biblical sources such as the Genesis account of God's assertion that it is not good for the human person to be alone (Gen 2:18). This suspicion took different forms in various historical eras, such as the nineteenth-century belief that those pushing the frontiers of habitation into desert zones in North America would end up reverting to an animal existence in the absence of human company.

Today the single greatest call that solitude makes to human beings is to create the space for attunement to the deep and true self, where God is at home in each one. Martin Laird aptly announces the invitation: "Let us journey home, then, to the silence of our own fathoms by becoming still."[14] John Michael Talbot, founder of the new monastic expression Little Portion Hermitage represents the silence-solitude-stillness interaction in the following manner:

> if we seek both external and interior silence, we must establish
> an environment where this deep silence can be developed and

13. Koch, *Solitude* 201–17.

14. Laird, *Into the Silent Land*, 6.

grow. This environment is solitude. When solitude and silence are joined together, they produce a sacred stillness that permeates every aspect of life.[15]

From within this stillness, it is possible discern the true guiding light of life, so poetically articulated by John of the Cross as the light "burned in my heart."[16]

However, gaining access to this deep true self faces new and ever more challenging obstacles with each new decade. The social construction of each person's identity is relentlessly advancing through the proliferation of cyber communities. Facebook, which was created in 2004, is eroding the time and capacity for solitude in a unique manner, as it sucks its users into the relentless accumulation of "friends" whom one will often never meet, and with whom one shares little more than the transitory incidents of life. One young insightful Facebook user recently noted that one of her pastimes was "wasting my life on Facebook." When time spent on this Internet site is combined with the pressures from text messaging and making Twitter comments, the challenges of disentangling the personal self from the public messaging self, so as to be embrace the true self in solitude, were never greater.[17] As William Deresiewicz has commented, "In our intensely networked culture we are tempted to live exclusively in relation to others, and we lose familiarity with that unique self that is encountered in solitude".

Since embracing solitude is not simply a matter of geographical isolation in a deserted place, or the withdrawal from the everyday demands of shopping, cooking, traveling, cleaning, working, and so on, but rather having the courage to strip off the mask of conventional living in favor of presenting to the world the true face of one's inner identity, it takes commitment to find this true self. In embracing solitude a person cultivates the practice of returning to the harbor of the heart, the inner home of being for which none but the true self possesses the entry code. Spiritual innovators such as Francis of Assisi have through the ages reflected on the geography of solitude and emphasized the cave of the heart as the true space of solitude even in busy lives;

> Although you are traveling, nevertheless, let your behavior be
> as decent as if you were staying in a hermitage or a cell because

15. Talbot, *The World Is My Cloister*, 21.

16. See *The Collected Works of St. John of the Cross*.

17. Deresiewicz, "The End of Solitude."

wherever we are or wherever we travel, we have a cell with us. Brother Body is our cell, and the soul is the hermit who remains inside the cell to pray to God and meditate. So if the soul does not remain in quiet and solitude in its cell, a cell made by hands does little good to a religious.[18]

In true solitude one finds one is attentive to a presence in one's inner core that may often be different from how others name one's personal essence. In solitude, the quieting of inner and outer critics allows one to let go of the egoic self and to become present to the most profound truth of one's being. Embracing solitude in this view involves moving to a place of healing, but it takes confidence and courage to be alone in the inner room of being. "In a world of noise, confusion and conflict," Merton wrote, "it is necessary that there be places of silence, inner discipline and peace; not the peace of mere relaxation but the peace of inner clarity and love based on ascetic renunciation."[19] Harvard leadership trainers Ronald Heifetz and Marty Linsky have proposed that to establish such a "safe harbor"

18. Armstrong et al., *Francis of Assisi: Early Documents*, 215: "The Assisi Compilation is either compiled in or around Assisi between c.1246 and 1260 or is the product of more clandestine compilatory practices in the decades following the decree from 1266 to destroy all hagiographical texts on Francis, except for the now official texts of Bonaventure": See Roest, "Francis and the Pursuit of Learning in Robson, *The Cambridge Companion to Francis of Assisi*, 161–77; quotation on 162.

19. This quote is from an essay Merton wrote that was originally published as *Come to the Mountain* (1964) and then subsequently as *Cistercian Life* (1974). The booklet is a kind of introduction to the monastic life for visitors or potential novices. This quote comes from the introduction (which is unpaginated) and is part of the following paragraph: "what matters about the monastery is precisely that it is radically different from the world. The apparent 'pointlessness' of the monastery in the eyes of the world is exactly what gives it a real reason for existing. In a world of noise, confusion, and conflict *it is necessary for there to be places of silence, inner discipline and peace: not the peace of mere relaxation but the peace of inner clarity and love based on ascetic renunciation.* In a world of tension and breakdown it is necessary for there to be men who seek to integrate their inner lives not by avoiding anguish and running away from problems, but by facing them in their naked reality and in their ordinariness! Let no one justify the monastery as a place from which anguish is utterly absent and in which men 'have no problems.' This is the myth, closely related to the other myth that religion itself disposes of all men's anxieties. Faith itself implies a certain anguish, and it is a way of confronting inner suffering, not a magic formula for making all problems vanish. It is not by extraordinary spiritual adventures or by dramatic and heroic exploits that the monk comes to terms with life. The monastery teaches men to take their own measure and to accept their ordinariness; in a word, it teaches them that truth about themselves which is known as 'humility.'" I greatly appreciate the collaboration of Dr Paul M Pearson, Director and Archivist, Thomas Merton Center, Bellarmine University in providing this information regarding the source of the quotation.

does not have to involve journeys to distant sanctuaries but rather can be found at "the kitchen table of a house, or a regular routine such a daily walk through the neighborhood.[20] Contemporary solitude is therefore intrinsically democratic.

Questions for Reflection / Journaling

- Where have my wanderings away from the hearth of my being taken me?

- What are the challenges I face in embracing the dispositions of solitude?

- What is of assistance to me in hearing the music of the Spirit—movement, music, poetry, gardening, dance, pottery, drawing, journaling?

- Have I experienced the power of pilgrimage in coming to know the journey of the heart?

- Where do I experience community without advice and answers, the willingness of others to witness to my human experience, struggle, and hope?

- How do I structure the two fundamental practices of solitude—stillness and awareness—into my daily life?[21]

- With whom do I share most deeply about my yearnings and struggles in pursuit of solitude?

---

20. Heifetz and Linsky, *Leadership on the Line*, 204–5.
21. Laird, *Into the Silent Land*, 4.

Reflection on New Monasticisms

"Monachesimo non è un contenitore; è un energia."
"Monasticism isn't a container; it's an energy."[1]

EMANUELE BARGELLINI, OSBCᴀᴍ

In my soul there is a temple, a shrine,
a mosque, a church where I kneel.[2]

RABIA

Iᴛ ɪs ᴀʟᴡᴀʏs ᴀɴ interesting experience to tell a story. Recently I noticed how personal an act storytelling can be. I spent an evening with a friend whom I only meet every couple years because she lives in the Philippines. There was much to share with her as the years since our last meeting had been exceptionally eventful. I found that at the end of our conversation, I had come to know my own life in a new way though the spontaneous act of selecting events, encounters, and experiences to share with her. In telling a story we organize our data within a horizon of meaning. In the same way, I turn now to reflect on new monasticisms. In telling my version of the story of new monasticisms, I know that I was meeting this phenomenon before I had a name for it.

My first sense of something new happening in terms of spiritualities of solitude came in 1995. I was researching the living spirituality of the

---

1. Emanuele Bargellini prior general OSBCam in conversation with Cyprian Consiglio OSBCam (Extract from public lecture by Cyprian to New Monasticism Ireland in Dublin, 20 November, 2010).

2. Ladinsky, translator, *Love Poems from God*, 11. I suggest that *monastery* could be added to Rabia's list.

long-term residents of Dublin's inner city, with a view to identifying effective pastoral strategies for inner-city ministry. When doing background reading for the research, I became aware of a great diversity of spiritual initiatives in urban settings. In particular, I became aware of new urban spiritualities of solitude emanating from groups. One in particular attracted my attention. The monastic Communities of Jerusalem, which were founded at Saint Gervais church in Paris on All Saints' Day 1975 by Père Pierre-Marie Delfieux, with Soeur Marie and with the support of Cardinal François Marty. While both men and women can join the community, there are significantly more women members. Their mission is to "work in the city, pray in the city, work and pray for the city, weep and sing with the city." Their life has five distinctive characteristics. In response to the growing phenomenon of global urbanization they have chosen to be city dwellers. They have not chosen to define the intentional practice of solitude in their lives by the enclosure of walls but seek instead to stay heart-centered. Their horarium is set by the rhythm of the comings and goings of the working population in the city rather than by the rhythm of light, which defined earlier forms of monasticism. They are committed to being wage earners as an act of solidarity with the city's mass of workers and so embrace solitude of heart in the workplace. Their fifth option is to be part of the diocesan Church, in the spirit of Vatican II, in order to live the intentional spirituality of solitude as a gift to the local Church.

Their Rule of Life[3] begins its reflection on the call to give expression to a living faith in the city with a quotation from the Acts of the Apostles: "Get up, enter the city and you will be told what to do" (Acts 9:6). It situates its hope in God's presence in the city not in any social or religious movement but in the multiple Scripture references to God's action in the city. It provides a foundation for its inspiration by establishing a correspondence between the characteristics of biblical cities and the modern city. The inclusion of the word *Jerusalem* within the title chosen for the community clearly aligns it within a particular strand of theology within the Hebrew Scriptures.

Some scholars conceive the Hebrew Scriptures as containing two distinct social traditions or streams of tradition. On the basis of George Mendenhall's historical evidence, Walter Brueggemann has drawn a theological profile of the two traditions:

3. Fraternités monastiques de Jérusalem, *A City Not Forsaken.*

> The Mosaic tradition tends to be a movement of protest situated among the disinherited and that articulates its theological vision in terms of a God who decisively intrudes, even against seemingly impenetrable institutions and orderings. On the other hand, the Davidic tradition tends to be a movement of consolidation situated among the established and secure and that articulates its theological vision in terms of a God who faithfully abides and sustains on behalf of the present ordering.[4]

Given this characterization of the two traditions Brueggemann designates the Mosaic tradition the "liberation" trajectory and the Jerusalem tradition the "royal" trajectory.[5] In distinguishing between these two strands the issue of justice is crucial. Brueggemann suggests that the royal trajectory of the Jerusalem tradition lacked an interest in justice because it was based in creation faith, which embraced "more of the imperial myths of the ancient Near East" and broke "with the scandalous historical particularity of the Moses tradition."[6] In a similar fashion the form of urban spirituality being developed by the Jerusalem community reflects an engagement with the universal and timeless love of God for the city, more than the particular and concrete phenomena of city living.

A second source of inspiration clearly evident in the rule of life of the Jerusalem community is that of the desert mothers and fathers. In using this lens this new monastic community has come to view the city as a contemporary desert, and they imagine the possible reversal of the spiritual movement from city to desert that third-century Christians initiated. This is because city and desert have now swapped the significance they had in those times. What defined a city in ancient times were its walls. The very word *city* (*'ir*) in Hebrew means "an enclosed place." Under attack, people fled their fields and villages and headed for the nearest city. The desert, on the other hand, was a place without walls, a place where demons roamed, a lonely place. To live in the desert was to live undefended, to expose oneself to the elements and sleep lightly. Today the city's walls have fallen in the vision of the Jerusalem communities. It is no longer a place to go to be safe but a place to go to be challenged, to wrestle with the contemporary demons of corruption and excess, as well as the beasts of homelessness and despair.

4. Brueggemann, "Trajectories in Old Testament Literature and the Sociology of Ancient Israel," 162.

5. Ibid., 163.

6. Ibid., 171.

While the Communities of Jerusalem at Saint Gervais are one of the best-known expressions of new urban monasticism in Europe, there are many other developments in a similar vein.[7] Among these other expressions of new urban monasticism, not all are communal. The eremitical strand is also well represented: for example in the case in the life of Hugette, who left behind a Carmelite cloister for a Brussels attic.[8] Like the life of the Jerusalem community, her way of life was deeply inspired by the life of the third-century desert hermits, since the anonymity that their desert hermitages provided was equally available to her in the immensity of the modern city.

As I consider such a manifestation of intentional spiritual seeking taking place in an innovative form today, my conviction is that insight of the distinguished Catholic religious thinker Raimundo Panikkar[9] regarding the "Monk as Universal Archetype" is making itself present in our midst in Western culture. In his book about the metaphorical and archetypal image of the monk,[10] Panikkar does not present the monk as a figure pursuing an idealized life form, but rather he discusses how the archetype of the monk represents a universal struggle of humanity to live from the deepest grounds of truth and authenticity, from the ground of naked presence to God. The monk pursues a radical lifestyle that may assume diverse forms in different historical eras, but for which abandonment to Divine mystery, attunement to the mystery of love, single-heartedness, alertness to the lessons of the natural world, and the embrace of a non-egoic path are central traits.

> The monk does not become a monk just because of a desire. He [sic] will be told time and again to eliminate all desires. I speak of an aspiration and an urge. it is not because one wills it that one becomes a monk. The monk is compelled, as it were, by an experience that can only articulate itself in the praxis of one's life . . . It is the existence of such an ontological aspiration in the

7. Landron, *Communautés Nouvelles.*

8. See Poleman, "Une vocation d'ermite," 341–51; and Gonyon, *Contemplative Sisters Living Outside the Monastery.*

9. Raimon Panikkar died on August 26, 2010, at the age of ninety-one, while this chapter was being written.

10. Panikkar, *Blessed Simplicity.* A useful brief introduction to this book is provided by Francis Tiso under the title "Raimundo Panikkar on the Monk as 'Archetype'" in the electronic journal *Dialogue Interreligieux Monastique / Monastic Interreligious Dialogue* (DIMMID), *Dilatato Corde* 1/2 (July–December) 2011). See http://www.dimmid.org/.

human being that leads me to speak of monkhood as a constitutive dimension of human life.[11]

Pannikar invites his readers to reflect on how a "new monk" may already be represented in our societies through all those who do not feel attracted to join traditional spiritual institutions but who nevertheless are attracted to embedding elements of monastic life in daily schedules.[12] In other words, not all those who feel called to go beyond what religious institutions normally provide for in terms of embracing solitude live in monasteries today.[13] Instead the archetype active in people may be found in all types of life circumstances where they aspires to reach the ultimate goal of life with all their being by renouncing all that is not necessary to it,: "In point of fact, the new monks are precisely those who contribute to the crystallization of the archetype."[14]

Since archetypes are symbolic forms and operate within the imaginal realm, it is worth considering the iconic significance for our present times of the choice of the recent papal name of Benedict, the founder of European monasticism. In line with Panikkar's vision then, I suggest that humanity may be witnessing an attraction to a "new monasticism." In other words, we are in the throes of the birth of a new expression of humanity's transcendent quest. On a wider level, Panikkar is suggesting that monasticism provides a unifying zone for contemplative commitment across religious traditions in an increasingly globalized world.

One of Panikkar's interlocutors at the conference[15] where he presented the papers now gathered in the publication *The Monk as Universal Archetype*, Professor Ewert Cousins, suggested that the universal human phenomenon to which the contemporary emergence of the monastic icon points is the development of a "universal" spirituality[16] (i.e., global spirituality). Global spirituality is characterized by a deep respect for the

11. Ibid 27.

12. Ibid. 28.

13. I will look at the manifestation of this phenomenon in literature, film, and TV documentary in more detail in the next chapter.

14. Tiso, "Raimundo Panikkar on the Monk as Archetype," 24.

15. The North American subcommission of Aide Inter Monastères, (a collaborative venture created by the Congress of Benedictine abbots meeting in Rome 1n 1959 for the provision of information and coordination relevant to the growth of monastic life outside the West) hosted the conference in 1980 in Holyoke, Massachusetts at which Raimundo Panikkar presented the concept of the monk as a universal archetype.

16. Panikkar, *Blessed Simplicity*, 138.

diversity of spiritual paths that different religions hold in trust. Monks have been to the fore in the exploration of the storehouse of contemplative practices of global spirituality, particularly through the mechanism of the Monastic Interreligious Dialogue,[17] which is sponsored by the Benedictine and Cistercian monasteries of North America. These dialogues have explored such themes such as *Transforming Suffering: Reflections on Finding Peace in Troubled Times* (2002) and *Simple and Sufficient: Monastic Spiritualities and the Environment* (2008).

The globally iconic monk Thomas Merton (1915–1968) anticipated in his own spiritual consciousness some of the evolution we are currently experiencing in a foundational religious experience, which is often perceived as one of the triggers for a new monasticisms. Merton uniquely captures the shift in spiritual consciousness involved in the development of new monasticism in a notable account of his own awakening, described in his book *Conjectures of a Guilty Bystander.*

> In Louisville, at the corner of Fourth and Walnut, in the center of the shopping district, I was suddenly overwhelmed with the realization that I loved all those people, that they were mine and I theirs, that we could not be alien to one another even though we were total strangers. It was like waking from a dream of separateness, of spurious self-isolation in a special world, the world of renunciation and supposed holiness. The whole illusion of a separate holy existence is a dream. Not that I question the reality of my vocation, or of my monastic life: but the conception of "separation from the world" that we have in the monastery too easily presents itself as a complete illusion.[18]

The monk is not however simply a passive icon of the contemporary spiritual quest. It also provides a vehicle for gathering contemporary spiritual awareness in an active, engaged, dynamic manner. I have in mind here the emergence of concrete expressions of what is variously called the "new monasticism," "monasticism without walls,"[19] "invisible

---

17. See http://www.monasticdialog.com/.

18. Merton, *Conjectures of a Guilty Bystander*, 156. First Published in 1966. The intersection of Fourth and Walnut Streets is now Fourth and Muhammad Ali Boulevard. A previous version of this experience was recorded by Merton in his private journal on March 19, 1958, the day after his fateful visit to Louisville and the seventeenth anniversary of his taking the vows of the Trappist order.

19. Keuss, "A Spirituality for The Advent City," 5–7; Main, *Monastery without Walls.*

monasticism,"[20] "portable monasticism,"[21] "secular monasticism,"[22] "lay monasticism,"[23] or "everyday monasticism."[24] Five generations in the emergence of such new monasticisms have been identified by Ray Simpson in *High Street Monasteries: Fresh Expression of Committed Christianity*.[25] While I don't divide the time line of the emergence in quite the same way as Ray Simpson, I have found his framework valuable, and below I set out my framework for understanding new monasticisms. This framework does not have the clear order of Carolus Linnaeus's botanical classification system, which grouped species according to shared physical characteristics, since "as a movement new monasticism is not coherent or unified; it operates in a low-key way, and generally at a grassroots level."[26] The outline below has not included some new expressions of monasticism such as scientific monasticism or pagan monasticism[27] as this reflection is located in the Christian tradition.

In the first generation of new expressions of monastic disciplines in daily life we find a number of people who personally came under the influence of Thomas Merton and his thinking. *Conjectures of a Guilty Bystander*, quoted above, is a collection of reflections by Thomas Merton that sought to provide a response to the terror of the world around him, the world he had been raised into, and the world he sought to leave behind as a monk in the back corners of Kentucky. Dorothy Day (1897–1980), founder of the Catholic Worker Movement, and Catherine de Hueck Doherty (1896–1985), author of the timeless best seller *Poustinia*[28] and founder of Friendship House in New York and Madonna House in Canada both belong to the group of new monastics who sought to bring to life monasticism's naked presence to God in the circumstances of social pov-

---

20. See http://digilander.libero.it/monast/inglese/index.htm/.

21. David Steindl-Rast OSB, http://www.gratefulness.org/readings/dsr_sacred Journey.htm/.

22. Anthony Grimley, MONOS, http://www.monos.org.uk/; Anthony Grimley tells the story of his family's journey in living a secular monastic vocation in Grimley and Wooding, *Living the Hours*, 157–77.

23. Plaiss, *The Inner Room*.

24. Fedorowicz, "Everyday Monasticism."

25. Simpson, *High Street Monasteries*.

26. Adams and Mobsby, "New Monasticism," in *Fresh Expressions in the Sacramental Tradition*, 52–65; quotation on 55.

27. See http://artmonastery.org/.

28. Doherty, *Poustinia: Encountering God in Silence, Solitude and Prayer*.

erty and alienation. In different ways each of these women recognized, like Merton, that the whole illusion of a separate holy existence is a dream. Complicated personal relationships, parenthood, and social activism come together in a new expression of monastic single-heartedness in each of their lives. For each of them the greatest challenge of the day was how to bring about a revolution of the heart, how to deepen personal authenticity and integrity in the mundane and challenging circumstances of broken relationships, failure, and great expectations.

In the lives of Dorothy Day and Catherine deHueck Doherty a certain blurring of the previously fixed lines of demarcation between a spiritually focused life, lived within monastic structures, and a spiritually focused life lived outside of such walls began to occur. A recognition of the necessary emergence of this blurring is present in the writings of another contemporary spiritual teacher, Pierre Teilhard de Chardin, SJ (1881–1955). In the context of his cosmic evolutionary vision he too saw the future as one involving a kind of rapprochement between human life as lived within monastic settings and human life lived outside monastery walls. In his 1927 work *Le Milieu Divin* (*The Divine Milieu*) he wrote:

> May the time come when men, having been awakened to a sense of the close bond linking all the movements of this world in the single, all-embracing work of the Incarnation, shall be unable to give themselves to any one of their tasks without illuminating it with the clear vision that their work—however elementary it may be—is received and put to good use by a Center of the universe. When that comes to pass, there will be little to separate life in the cloister from life in the world.[29]

World War II is the context for a second wave of new experimentation with monasticism. Brother Roger (1915–2005) who sowed the seeds of Taizé, and Chiara Lubich (1920–2008), who founded Focolare both established their communities of reconciliation and inclusion within an environment of war, distrust, and violence. Both have been recognized for their contributions to integrating interreligious dialogue and understanding into their new expressions of monastic living. One of the most significant documents from this second wave of new expressions of monasticism has perhaps however been provided by the Lutheran pastor Dietrich Bonhoeffer (1906–1945) in his book *The Cost of Discipleship.*[30]

29. Teilhard de Chardin, *The Divine Milieu*, 67.
30. Bonhoeffer, *The Cost of Discipleship.* The original book was written in 1937.

Prior to this book, Bonhoeffer had expressed his conviction that authentic Christian living required uncompromising integrity in a new manner. This insight arose for him from the unique challenges he encountered in living Christianity under the political oppression of the Third Reich. In a letter to his brother Karl-Friedrich in 1935 he asserted: "The restoration of the church must surely come only from a new type of monasticism . . . I think it is time to gather people together to do this."[31] Bonhoeffer, who had to surrender his life to executioners in order to live what he described to his brother as "a life lived in accordance with the Sermon on the Mount," struggled to enact his vision of a radical Protestant Christian community. When he became director of a seminary for the Confessing Church, which was founded to oppose the collusion of the official German Protestant churches with Nazism, Bonhoeffer had the opportunity to work out his new monasticism vision concretely with six ordinands. Central to his vision was the conviction that impersonal adherence to christological dogmas would not be sufficient to sustain those who confronted the violence of the dispensation in which they found themselves. Naked presence to Christ must be cultivated: "Discipleship means adherence to Christ, and because Christ is the object of that adherence, it must take the form of discipleship. An abstract Christology, a doctrinal system, a general religious knowledge on the subject of grace or the forgiveness of sins, render discipleship superfluous."[32]

Bonhoeffer's inspiration reverberated synchronically as well as diachronically. Synchronised with his efforts to promote radical gospel living in Germany were the efforts of George McLeod (1895–1991), founder of the Iona Community in Scotland in 1938. While Ronald Ferguson, the biographer of George MacLeod, has not located published evidence of influence of Bonhoeffer's 1935 vision, he does believe that MacLeod was familiar with it.[33] MacLeod was a Church of Scotland pastor who organized out-of-work stonemasons and carpenters in Glasgow to rebuild the abbey on the island of Iona. His dream was to close the gap between work and worship by integrating a busy, active life with a rhythm of awareness of God at work in all dimensions of daily involvement.

In considering the diachronic influence of Bonhoeffer it is useful to openthewebsiteoftheNorthumbriacommunity(http://www.northumbria

---

31. De Grouchy, *Bonhoeffer for a New Day*, 48.

32. Ibid. 50.

33. Ferguson, *George McLeod*, 140.

community.org), which has its headquarters in northeast England and was founded in the early 1990s.[34] On the website of the Northumbria community you will find that its story begins with Bonhoeffer's vision. Combined with this vision are practical monastic inspirations from a new expression of ecumenical Benedictine life at Rosin in Scotland, which was founded 1965 with the support of the Anglican bishop of Edinburgh and the Roman Catholic abbot of Nunraw, as well as with inspiration from the legacy of Clonfert in Ireland, the site of the sixth-century monastery of St. Brendan the Navigator. The daily office prayerbook produced by the Northumbria community gives notable prominence to the lives and teachings of early Irish saints.[35] In their rule of life the community emphasizes that they seek to embrace and express the heart of monastic spirituality by living the virtues of *availability* and *vulnerability* in the everyday ordinariness of life and in this way to make a difference in the competitive, aggressive, and violent culture so prevalent today.

The diachronic influence of Bonhoeffer is also evident in the Community of the Transformation at Geelong, Victoria, Australia. The Community of the Transfiguration was established in the early 1970s. This Baptist community's founders, Graeme Littleton and Steven Shipman, combined the influence of Bonhoeffer with the vision of Gordon and Mary Cosby. The latter had established the Church of the Savior in Washington DC as an expression of the compassionate insight nurtured in Gordon while he served as a chaplain in World War II. As Cosby preached and talked with young soldiers, many of whom would die imminently, he had dreamt of a community that would prepare its members to live lives fully committed to Christ.[36] Bonhoeffer's writings provided practical guidance for translating the Washington vision into an Australian context.

A third strand of new monasticism—independent from the influences of Merton or Bonhoeffer—has created its identity by forming new partnerships and associations with living traditional monastic communities. The groups emerging under this heading have a strong association with classical monastic rules such as those lived by the Carthusians, Cistercians, or Benedictines. The strong positive reception in 2005 of the BBC Two documentary *The Monastery*, filmed with the Benedictine

34. The Lindisfarne Community, founded in 1996, also has its roots in the North East of England. See J. Hall Fitz-Gibbon and A. Fitz-Gibbon, *Secular Monasticism.*

35. The Northumbria Community, *Celtic Daily Prayer.*

36. O'Connor, *Call to Commitment.*

community of Worth Abbey, England,[37] showed clearly that the call to creative solitude and contemplative attentiveness are no longer viewed as life commitments solely for cloistered monks and nuns; rather these practices are now appreciated as the lifeblood of committed intentional spiritual seekers. Yet in order to be true to the spiritual quest in the rush of modern living, many know they need the support of other people on the same journey and the sensible advice of wise, experienced guides.

An article by the Welsh spirituality scholar, Esther de Waal, which is titled "Living with a Monastic Heart,"[38] gives typical voice to how the new monasticism of this variety involves living the classical rules of life in daily life settings. In de Waal's case it is the Benedictine rule that shaped her married life. She says:

> It [The Rule of Benedict] spoke to me of things I have struggled with in my own life: how to hold a family together because a family and a community have got so much in common; how to handle the ordinary things in life and make these a way to God; . . . how to keep the open door of hospitality and a warm welcome to everyone who comes, without allowing myself to be exhausted by the constant pressure of people. And in all of this how to find time and space for prayer while living a very ordinary, practical, day-to-day life.[39]

Jane Tomaine, the American author of *St. Benedict's Toolbox: The Nuts and Bolts of Everyday Benedictine Living*,[40] echoes de Waal's conviction of the capacity of the Benedictine rule to facilitate living with greater depth and presence in daily life. Hospitality is one of the instruments within the Benedictine toolbox that is particularly challenging for Tomaine also. For her hospitality counters the overprivatization of family life, and its practice raises questions regarding how to extend homeliness beyond the confines of the biological family, including situations where this challenge arises in an unplanned manner. Living monastic hospitality in family life also provokes reflection on practices for honoring the Christ presence at meals; not an inconsiderable challenge in these times of TV dinners and microwave suppers.[41]

37. The teaching of the program series is distilled in Jamison, *Finding Sanctuary*.

38. De Waal, "Living with a Monastic Heart" in Whelan, *Issues for Church and Society in Australia*.

39. See http://www.celticpilgrimage.org/estherbenedict.htm/.

40. Tomaine, *St. Benedict's Toolbox*.

41. Ibid. 132–38.

Many other female writers have translated the wisdom learned in the company of contemporary monastic communities into the public square. Susan Stevenot Sullivan is a lay Cistercian who has reflected on how the reign of God may be in a new stage of establishment through the diversity of people being called to embed the detachment of monastic practices in lives increasingly under consumerist pressures.[42] Janet Buchanan, an associate of the Methodist Benedictine monastery of St. Brigid of Kildare in Minnesota, has collated her extensive research under the title "Monks beyond Monastery Walls: Benedictine Oblation and the Future of Benedictine Spirituality." It is her contention that the views of Raimundo Panikkar as well as the ideas of Marsha Sinetar,[43] who both witness to the global emergence of forms of intentional spiritual commitment in daily life in a regulated form, point to the emergence of new monks.[44] Kathleen Norris,[45] Cynthia Bourgeault,[46] Norvene Vest,[47] and Beverly Lanzetta[48] have also made significant contributions to translating traditional monastic wisdom into daily life commitments and practices.

Among the structures of classical monasticism which have been translated into new settings in the new monasticism movement is the skete arrangement. This approach to sharing support in the spiritual journey can be traced back to the Egyptian desert monastic movement. The arrangement consists in the geographical clustering of those on a common spiritual journey. Philip Roderick has described it as "connected solitude,"[49] a mechanism of dispersed protection and support for

42. Sullivan, "How Can This Be?," 26–31.

43. Sinetar, *Ordinary People as Monks and Mystics*.

44. Unpublished DMin diss., 1999, Graduate Theological Foundation of Donaldson, Indiana . Further data on the oblate expression of new monasticism, particularly its ecumenical dimensions, is available in Kulzer and Bondi, *Benedict in the World*.

45. Norris, *The Cloister Walk*. This is a reflection on the impact of participation in the life of the Benedictine St John's Abbey Minnesota on the daily life of the author.

46. Bourgeault, *Love Is Stronger Than Death*. This is a record of how a monk at St Benedict's Monastery, Snowmass, Colorado, and the author collaborate in the monastic work of total inner transformation.

47. Vest, *Desiring Life*. This book is the third in a series of books by Vest regarding living the practices of monastic life in daily settings based on her own experiences as a Benedictine oblate. The other books are *No Moment Too Small*; and *Friend of the Soul*.

48. Lanzetta, *Emerging Heart*. Beverly made profession of vows as a contemplative monk in 2001: her monastic vision is deeply influenced by the work of Raimondo Panikkar.

49. Roderick, "Connected Solitude: Re-Imagining the *Skete*" in Cray et al., *New*

those on a common journey. This skete model has profoundly influenced Roderick, who has recently been developing an adapted skete model in his Hidden House of Prayer initiative. He is seeking to nurture "an invisible network of people drawn to the practice of contemplative, creative and intercessory prayer in their own homes."[50]

A fourth strand of new monasticism is also associated with translating historical monastic traditions into daily life, but in this case the tradition does not have current living loci since the tradition in question is the Celtic monastic tradition. The distinctive Irish version of Celtic monasticism began coming to an end in 1117—after Ireland had seeded monasteries all over Europe—when the English king Henry II, supported by the English pope Hadrian IV, invaded Ireland for the purpose of reforming the native monastic system of the Church so as to secure its alignment with the Roman diocesan style. One of the most developed new monastic expression of Celtic monasticism is the Community of Aidan and Hilda, a group established by the Anglican priest Ray Simpson. In 1985 he visited the ancient monastic site of the Holy Island of Lindisfarne for the first time. It was here that St Aidan, who had formerly lived at Iona, established one of the first Christian communities in Anglo-Saxon England. On New Year's Eve 1987, while again visiting Holy Island, Ray experienced a call by God to explore a New Way in the church inspired by the monastic-community way of life of the Celtic church. The Community of Aidan and Hilda, which is named after two significant saints of the Celtic church active in creating Christian communities in the northeast of England in the seventh century, welcomes married and unmarried Christians from across the denominational spectrum.[51]

Not all new monastic groups who trace their spiritual roots to a Celtic inspiration are based at Celtic sites. The Prayer Foundation, a prayer ministry service, has developed a monastic order, the Knights of Prayer, which is advertised as "the first Born-Again Christian Monastic Order".[52] It was founded in March 1999 in Vancouver, Washington State, after S. G. Preston and his wife, Linda, had visited Ireland and Assisi. As

Monasticism as Fresh Expression of Church, 102–19.

50. Ibid. 114. Hidden Houses of Prayer is a partnership project between three initiatives of Philip Roderick; Contemplative Fire, The Quiet Garden Movement, and Whirlow Grange Spirituality Centre in Sheffield, UK.

51. Simpson, "Celtic Monastic Inheritance and New Monasticism," in Cray et al., *New Monasticism as Fresh Expression of Church*, 120–30.

52. An interview article with this group appeared in the Ideas section of *The Boston Globe* newspaper on Feb. 3, 2008: Molly Worthen, "The Unexpected Monks."

well as the Celtic influence, there is evidence of Franciscan and Carmelite sources in the group's website (www.prayerfoundation.org/), including a recommendation of the Carmelite Brother Lawrence (Nicholas Herman, c. 1605–1691) classic titled *The Practice of the Presence of God.*[53] The fact that the original members of the Celtic and Franciscan movements were missionary makes such traditions attractive to the ministry of Protestant evangelicals today. The way of life of the group is encapsulated in a "Celtic Cross Rule of Seven": *One Desire* "Draw near to God, and He will draw near to you." (James 4:8); *Two Devotions* (Prayer and Scripture) and *Four Goals* (Right Life, Right Belief, Right Practice, Right Ministry).

Another expression of new monasticism with Celtic and Franciscan influences is the Franciscan Order of Céli Dé. It began in October of 1992 as the Brotherhood of St. Francis. In 1994 the name was changed to the Franciscan Order of Céli Dé (FOCD) and it opened its membership to women. The FOCD. has two communities: the Gray Friars for men and the Sisters of Brigit and Clare for women.[54] Members may be married or single. It has been incorporated as an autocephalus order under the guidelines of Canon 30 of the Episcopal Church USA. James Aidan Ketlern was the founder and is the current elected abbot of the FOCD.[55] The Rule of St. Francis, written in 1221 (*Regulla non-Bullato*),[56] and the teachings of the Celtic saints inform the way of life.[57]

---

53. Brother Lawrence, *The Practice of the Presence of God.*

54. The Rule of life of the group may be viewed online: http://dfba.home.mind spring.com/celide.html/.

55. In ninth-century Ireland a new version of monasticism called Céli Dé developed in several locations. It acted as a spiritual reform movement within traditional Irish monasticism. Oengus was one of its most notable exponents, and after he died in Tallaght (south of Dublin), Maelrun who had shared life with him for some time drew up a rule of life for the group. This Tallaght monastery became the headquarters of the Ceilí Dé (also known as Culdees, or the servants of God).

56. In its early stages of foundation, the organizational sophistication of the disciples of Francis of Assisi did not keep up with its growth, and the movement had little more to govern it than Francis's example and simple rule. To address this problem, Francis prepared a new and more detailed rule, the "First Rule" or "Rule without a Bull" (*Regula prima, Regula non bullata*), which affirmed the characteristic devotion to poverty and the apostolic life.

57. Other new monastic communities influenced by the Celtic monastic heritage are the Lindisfarne Community of Ithaca, New York (http://www.icmi.org/home.html/); the Ark Community of Northriding, South Africa (http://www.thearkcommunity .org/); and Céile Dé, Kippen, Scotland (http://www.ceilede.co.uk/).

A fifth expression of contemporary monasticism without walls focuses on the arts as a key resource in nurturing contemplative consciousness. This expression has a tangible embodiment in the work of Christine
Valters Paintner, who has developed the online monastery Abbey of the
Arts.[58] Christine's model of monasticism is informed by the Catholic
mystical tradition and is rooted in her oblate membership of St. Placid's
Priory, a women's Benedictine monastic community in Lacey, Washington State. In her approach to working with the arts, she places a strong
emphasis on the process of artistic expression rather than the product of
artistic endeavors. She promotes a great variety of art modalities for contemplative practice, including photography, poetry, visual art, music and
movement. The notable spiritual innovator Richard Rohr, OFM, in his
testimonial on the website of the Abbey of the Arts notes that "Christine
is offering us a 'moving monastery' yet with solid grounding in Scripture,
Nature, Art, the Tradition, and the Saints. Abbey of the Arts is spirituality
for our time and every time."

Ian Adams, the founder of mayBe community[59] in Oxford, England,
also communicates his new monastic vision in poetry, art, photography,
and music. His book, *Cave, Refectory, Road: Monastic Rhythms for Contemporary Living* introduces each of twelve foundation stones for new
monastic communities in an evocative original poetic statement. On
"monastic learning practices and becoming more (beauty) fully human
in the way of Jesus," he reflects:

> I thought I was dead;
> Lost
> in the dark damp earth
> buried
> unknowing
>
> but in the deep
> you were forming me
> a seed planted
> tended
> loved
> awaited
> becoming[60]

58. See http://abbeyofthearts.com/.

59. See http://maybe.org.uk/.

60. Adams, "Lost" in *Cave, Refectory, Road*, 50, reprinted by permission of Canterbury Press.

A sixth strand of new monasticism is evident in European countries that are not associated with strong religious affiliation today, such as the Nordic countries. A new attraction to monasticism is emerging as a carrier of the contemporary religious quest in these highly detraditionalized societies. One expression of this attraction is the Integral Monastery,[61] which seeks to be an outreach to the many people today who, often despite enjoying great success in industrially advanced countries, still feel as if something is missing. Dawid Dahl from Stockholm, Sweden, has organized the Integral Monastery as a collaborative of urban monks who seek to integrate a challenging spirituality with the complexities of a technologically advanced society. The spirituality of the group is grounded in the Rule of Benedict and biblical texts such as the call of the rich young man (Mark 10:21). The commitments of the integral monk emphasise selflessness, that is shifting the focus of life *"From self, to God; From self, to others; From self, to life."* This monastery is at an early stage of development and does not yet have contemporary links to other equivalent developments.

Sweden is also home to another unique new expression of monasticism—one based in a prison. At Kumla, which is in central Sweden and is the location of one of Sweden's three high-security prisons, there is a special custodial division called the Monastery.[62] This space was opened in 2003 by a Lutheran minister and a Jesuit priest. At the Monastery prisoners may participate in a silent retreat in the Ignatian tradition. The aim of this Monastery project is to facilitate prisoners gain the courage to stop pretending and to dare to see both themselves and reality clearly. Some of those who have experienced this immersion in spiritual practice requested to live with others on the same journey of transformation. Thus the Christian Brotherhood of Saint Andrew was born, which has a monastic house at Skänninge Prison in South Sweden. Lysanne Sizoo captures the spirit of this initiative in a quote from an interview with one of the community residents: "I have behaved in a way that led to me losing my freedom. But I have found a new inner freedom. And I am, because of the monastic house in Skänninge, able to deepen that inner freedom, and grow stronger in myself."[63]

61. See http://www.integralmonastery.com/.

62. Sizoo, "When Cell Doors Close and Hearts Open," 161–68; and Sizoo, "Kumla Prison Monastery," 93–104.

63. Ibid 104.

Aware of the sheer abundance and diversity of manifestations of new monasticism, Julian Collette, a student at Saint John's School of Theology in Collegeville, Minnesota—in a project titled Emerging Communities: Ancient Roots—took to the road in the USA on a bicycle in January 2011 to seek out expressions of new monasticism that may be as hidden as that which is happening in Kumla Prison.[64] From his intereview conversations in various settings he distilled key characteristics of these emerging spiritual communities. In his third interview, which took place with Mary Ewing Stamps, leader of the Methodist-Benedictine Saint Brigid of Kildare Monastery,[65] structural elements were emphasized, such as a unique location, a designated convenor, an agreed way of life, and access to a shared teaching experience in a group's own home location. Another interviewee, the Camaldolese-Benedictine monk Cyprian Consiglio, speaking from within the eremitical (hermit) tradition and from years of involvement in monastic interreligious dialogue, named committed, integrated contemplative practice as the core of new monastic endeavors. In another interview with the Cistercian monk Michael Lautieri, the vocation director of Monastery of the Holy Spirit in Conyers, Georgia, the conversation highlighted the benefits of core members of neomonastic communities spending time with other neomonastic groups to explore how constitutive elements of any form of monastic spirituality (such as prayer, silence, solitude, work, and community) are integrated into the spirituality of the group. Michael Lautieri holds the conviction that the future of traditional monastic communities lies in stronger bonds with laypeople whose interests in monastic spirituality are contributing to deepening the spirituality in the traditional living of monastic values and practices.

Among the personally selected collage of living new expressions of the monastic impulse in the USA presented by Julian Collette, there was one interview which stood out as being the most moving for him—the encounter with the founder of Rutba House.[66] Shortly before the United States began bombing Iraq in 2003, a young college student, Jonathan Wilson-Hartgrove (1980–), and his new wife, Leah, traveled there as members of a Christian Peacemaker Team determined to tell Iraqis that

64. See http://emerging-communities.com/.

65. Much of Mary's own formation took place in a Benedictine monastic guest program similar to that offered by Monastery of the Holy Spirit, Conyers, Georgia.

66. Episode 26—Jonathan Wilson-Hartgrove of Rutba House: Family Economics in the Household of God, 28 June 2012. Online: http://emerging-communities.com/2012/06/.

American Christians did not all support the war. Their experiences became the subject of a book titled *To Baghdad and Beyond*.[67] In this book they tell the story of their ultimate conversion to the implicit reality of new monasticism when they experienced extended hospitality in the village of Rutba in Iraq after the jeep in which they were traveling had an accident.[68] On their return home they set up Rutba House, a local neighborhood monastic community where members pray, eat, and live monastic hospitality in the setting of their own homes.

A significant influence on Jonathan's turn to monastic spirituality values for the purpose of expressing full-hearted gospel living in daily life was his father-in-law, Jonathan R. Wilson. The latter had refreshed the contemporary usage of the term "new monasticism" in his 1997 book, *Living Faithfully in a Fragmented World: Lessons from MacIntyre's "After Virtue."*[69] Jonathan R. Wilson had Alasdair MacIntyre as a philosophy lecturer in class at Duke University while undertaking undergraduate studies there. MacIntyre had published an internationally acclaimed reconsideration of the foundations of ethics in a capitalist economy, and in the inspirational conclusion to this book titled *After Virtue*,[70] he issued a remedy for restoring a conscience to Western culture:

> What matters at this stage is the construction of local forms of community within which civility and the intellectual and moral life can be sustained through the new dark ages which are already upon us. And if the tradition of the virtues was able to survive the horrors of the last dark ages, we are not entirely without grounds for hope. This time however the barbarians are not waiting beyond the frontiers; they have already been governing us for some time. And it is our lack of consciousness of this that constitutes part of our predicament. We are waiting not for a Godot, but for another—doubtless very different—St. Benedict.[71]

---

67. Wilson-Hartgrove, *To Baghdad and Beyond*.

68. Jonathan had the seeds of a turn toward new monasticism initially sown through his visits to the Simple Way community which had been founded in Philadelphia, Pennysylvania, in 1997 by Shane Claiborne (1975–).

69. Wilson, *Living Faithfully in a Fragmented World*, 68–77.

70. MacIntyre, *After Virtue*.

71. Ibid, 2nd ed., 263

The sheer explosion of groups identifying with the new monastic impulse—the Simple Way, led by Shane Claiborne in Philadelphia;[72] the Nehemiah Community in Springfield, Massachusetts;[73] the Mennonite-affiliated Reba Place Fellowship in Evanston, Illinois;[74] the Winnipeg-based Little Flowers Community;[75] Barbara Hazzard's, "*urban monastery*"—Hesed in Oakland, California,[76] developed from the inspiration of John Main's Christian Meditation work; Living Stone Monastery[77] in Virginia, which lives as a community of evangelical Protestants committed to day and night prayer; Clarence Jordan's Koinonia Farm[78] community in Georgia—and many other establishments in North American witness to the deep search among contemporary people for networks of support for gospel living that embraces all of life.[79]

Those who have been on this journey for some time, such as John Michael Talbot of Little Portion Hermitage (founded in 1982) testify to fact that "the new monasticism encounters all the same challenges of new monastic expression from times past"[80]—it is not a utopian ideal. Publications and websites in the UK indicated that there is an equal abundance of new expressions of the fundamental monastic impulse there[81] with equally diverse new challenges.

Finally, some of the expressions of new monasticism reflect emerging new frontiers in spirituality such as ecospiritualty and interspirituality. In the former category, an initiative such as Green Mountain Monastery[82] identifies itself as the sixth major epochal expression of monasticism (the

72. See http://www.thesimpleway.org/.

73. See http://www.nehemiah-ministries.com/.

74. See http://www.rebaplacefellowship.org/; see Varela, "Reba Place Fellowship: Portrait of a New Monastic Community" in Kruschwitz, *Monasticism Old and New*, 69–76.

75. See http://littleflowers.ca

76. See http://www.hesedcommunity.org; Manss et al., "Lay Contemplative Formation Sites," in Manss and Frohlich, *The Lay Contemplative* 113–83; quotation from 128ff.

77. See http://www.livingstonemonastery.org/.

78. See http://www.koinoniapartners.org/.

79. A comprehensive listing may be found in Janzen, *The Intentional Christian Community Handbook*. A helpful descriptive introduction to some UK examples is provided in Cross, *Totally Devoted*.

80. Talbot, *The Universal Monk*, 46.

81. Croft and Mobsby, *Ancient Faith, Future Mission*. See http://new-monasticism -network.ning.com/.

82. See http://www.greenmountainmonastery.org/.

six are as follows: desert, community, mendicant, intellectual, activist, planetary/cosmological) and therefore as a necessary and fundamental development in monasticism's form for this time of ecological concern. The community vision is built on Thomas Berry's theory of the emergent Ecozoic Era,[83] through which Berry asserts that the foundations of community in the future will be born from a shared Christ consciousness.

In the interspiritual variety of new monasticism,[84] the foundations of community are built on the spiritual wisdom of multiple religious traditions. A significant figure for this form of new expression of monasticism is Wayne Teasdale (1945–2004),[85] for whom the image of the "mystic heart" captured his vision.[86] Through this image Teasdale emphasized that the encounters between religions today must, for the well-being of humanity, go beyond an intellectual connection to an encounter where the direct mystical experience of reality is known together. The inter-spiritual vision of new monasticism inspires the work of Rory McEntee and Adam Bucko, as they express it in the Foundation for New Monasticism. They aim to bring the new-monastic vision onto campuses through cultivating an interspiritual contemplative fellowship for college students under the name of the Hebrew word *hab* as well as establishing an expression of Bede Griffth's vision in the West.[87]

What the accounts of new monasticisms told above seem to indicate is that—echoing Ivan Illich[88]—neither renewal nor reform nor reconfiguration can ultimately change the situation of decline in many communities that were the homes of those on a spiritual journey in the past. Rather today communities with a commitment to live from a contemplative vision of God at work in our world must speak with new, more powerful metaphors, ones so persuasive that they melt away the old images and

83. Swimme and Berry, *The Universe Story.*

84. The vision of InterSpirituality evolved from the founding of the Christian-Hindu Shantivanum Ashram in India with its contemplative pioneers such as Fr. Jules Monchanin (aka Swami Parah Arubi Ananda); Fr. Roberto de Nobili, SJ; Fr. Henri Le Saux, OSB (aka Swami Abhishiktananda); and Fr. Bede Griffiths OSB (aka Swami Dayananda). Wayne Teasdale spent time at Shantivanum.

85. Teasdale, *The Mystic Heart*; and Teasdale, *A Monk in the World.*

86. See http://www.communityofthemysticheart.org/.

87. Jamie Manson, a reporter with the *National Catholic Reporter,* did a three-part report on the work of Rory and Adam in 2012 under the titles "Two Young Adults Offer a New Take on 'New Monasticism'"; "New Monasticism: Envisioning Monks without Borders"; "The Spiritual Hunger of Young Adults: Where Does It Come from and What Might They Need?". The articles are part of a series Grace on the Margins

88. See quotation in Viola, *From Eternity to Here,* 22.

offer recognition to the common call to holiness—metaphors so inclusive that they gather the past and shine light into the future, so that all who hear the call of God standing at the door knocking (Rev 3:20) can take one step forward together. The metaphors of monks, and monasteries, central to the new-monasticism impulse, seem to offer a trustworthy guiding beacon in a sea of spiritual complexity.

Questions for Reflection / Journaling

- What expressions of the renewed spiritual quest today have I encountered?
- What has given me pause for thought in such new expressions?
- Which authors are of assistance to me in hearing the voices of the new spiritual quest today?
- Have I a personal attraction to any of the elements of the spiritual journey being emphasised in the new spiritual quest?
- In the wealth of resources for contemplative practice in the Christian tradition, what have I recently experienced in a new way?
- How have I been personally challenged to renewal by the new universal call to holiness?
- How has my spiritual community / prayer group / parish been personally challenged to renewal by the new universal call to holiness?

Reflection on New Trends in Religious Experience in the West

THE THE QUEST FOR solitude, and its associated monaastic/contemplative practices, in today's Western societies is grounded in a wider shift in religious sensibility. There are many ways to explore this shift in spiritual experience in today's Western society. Studies like Paul Heelas's investigations of the living practice of religion in the small English village of Kendal, titled *The Spiritual Revolution*[1] or David Tacey's study *The Spirituality Revolution*,[2] which look at the surge of interest in spiritual practices internationally, immediately suggest themselves. While Woodhead and Tacey essentially affirm the awakening interest in forms of spiritual practices often based on personal enrichment and well-being, there are also other less enthusiastic voices. *Selling Spirituality: The Silent Takeover of Religion*[3] by Jeremy Carrette and Richard King explores the ways that the new public interest in the arts of spiritual practice is being exploited for commercial gain

Given the excellent sociological and philosophical resources available regarding current trends in Western religious experience,[4] I would prefer to reflect on this phenomenon through a different lens: that of metaphor. An appreciation is growing that just as science has always been understood through metaphorical language (yes, numbers are metaphors), so spirituality can also be understood through metaphorical figures of speech. In his book *The Audacity of Spirit*[5] Jack Finnegan has identified the task of becoming familiar with the language of metaphor as one of the central challenges for those hoping to discern the meaning of

1. Heelas et al., *The Spiritual Revolution*.
2. Tacey, *The Spirituality Revolution*.
3. Carrette and King, *Selling Spirituality*.
4. Boeve, *Interrupting Tradition*; Taylor, *A Secular Age*.
5. Finnegan, *The Audacity of Spirit*.

the variety of modalities in which contemporary spirituality is expressed: "metaphors help us speak about those thin places where the sacred hovers tantalisingly just beyond our fingertips . . . metaphor, the mother tongue of poetry, is also the mother tongue of spirituality."[6]

Poets and spirituality scholars are not alone in recognizing metaphor as a privileged communication medium in the current cultural climate. Indeed, engaging the evocative power of metaphor was a central strategy in Barack Obama's first presidential campaign. In March 2007 Barack Obama gave a speech commemorating the Selma Voting Rights March led by Dr. Martin Luther King Jr. in 1965. In this speech Obama acknowledged the life opportunities he had enjoyed because of what had been achieved by King and his associates:

> I'm here because somebody marched. I'm here because you all sacrificed for me. I stand on the shoulders of giants. I thank the Moses generation; but we've got to remember, now, that Joshua still had a job to do. As great as Moses was, despite all that he did, leading a people out of bondage, he didn't cross over the river to see the Promised Land. God told him, "your job is done. You'll see it. You'll be at the mountain top and you can see what I've promised . . . You'll see that I've fulfilled that promise but you won't go there."[7]

Obama went on to tease out the analogy: the Moses of today are invited to support the Joshua generation in order to make sure that great change happens again. The "Joshua generation" metaphor that Barack Obama popularized is perhaps a useful focus when reflecting on the subject of spiritual experience in today's Western society. As we consider the Moses era giving way to the Joshua era, we think of change, letting go and embracing the new. We are reminded that God is constantly made present in new ways in each generation, and that those who accompany others in the spiritual journey must be able to notice the new ways of the Spirit in new times.

Elijah is a biblical character who exemplifies how attentiveness, contemplative presence to the circumstances of his life, and willingness to embrace the unexpected were central to his alertness to God's presence around him. The account of Elijah's journey is full of metaphors

---

6. Finnegan, *The Audacity of the Spirit*, 119.

7. "Sen. Barack Obama Delivers Remarks at a Selma Voting Rights Commemoration," Washington Transcript Service, March 4, 2007.

with contemporary resonances.[8] Elijah had become accustomed to visible, concrete signs of God's presence in his life and in his society. Circumstances changed and Elijah began to despair. He fled the change of circumstances and undertook a long journey through a deserted, barren land, which led him into great despair. He came to the point when he could journey no further and stopped to rest with no support except that supplied by a bush. There, as the outward journey was suspended, he moved inward and put words on the wound in his heart: "I am no better than my ancestors" (1 Kgs 19:4). He grew into a realization that he had become rigid in his perception of how God can be at work in the circumstances of life, especially in his association of God's action with specific visible signs and supports.

Having acknowledged aloud the cry of his heart, he eventually continued his journey and arrived at Mount Horeb, an ancestral holy place. There Elijah underwent a profound transformation in his religious sensibility. In the past he had been familiar with the awesome palpable presence of God in fire, earthquake, and mighty winds, but there on Horeb he came to know the God of the gentle breeze. He crossed a threshold in his perception of the mode of God's presence with him—and with the society in which he lived. In crossing this threshold, he came home to a forgotten spiritual tradition where characters such as Adam and Eve had encountered the presence of God in the cool breeze during an evening garden walk.

Another biblical metaphor that may be helpful for discerning the monastic/contemplative quest of today's society is the Pentecost event. In this event the confusion that speaking different languages had created at the tower of Babel (Gen 11:1–7) is overcome. Parthians, Medes, and Elamites all hear the gospel proclaimed through the medium of their own languages. As we look at the diverse expressions of spirituality today, the choice again is to live in the alienation of Babel or the dialogical spirit of Pentecost. The ability to learn the language of the Spirit as it spoken in the spiritual metaphors of our culture today confronts each of us as profoundly

. . . as yielding to Joshua challenged Moses

. . . as recognizing the presence of God in the gentle breeze on Horeb challenged Elijah

and

. . . as the Pentecost event shattered the Jewish-only world within which the apostles had lived up to that time.

8. 1 Kings 19.

Using the work of the language theorist Noam Chomsky, the founders of Neuro-linguistic programming created a metamodel[9] that has identified three unhelpful processes by which each of us may be tempted to block out the constantly new data that the real world around us is generating: the processes of deletion, generalization, and distortion. Deletion can manifest itself when we exclude from our circle of familiarity the spiritual interests, readings, and movements of those who are different from each of our own particular views of the nature of spiritual commitment. Generalizations about contemporary emergent discipleship like, "it's very individualistic"; or, "they won't be able for the long haul," can short-circuit the conversation traditional spiritual communities need to have about the facts regarding the emergent diverse expressions of a new monasticism. Last, the tendency toward distortion can result in refusing to see any possibility for good in a tentatively emerging framework for the future. This is something I experienced recently in an e-mail requesting that I make no mention of Thomas Merton in writing or teaching about new solitude movements since in the view of the e-mail author Merton was nothing more than an alcoholic, a narcissist, and a sexual predator.

For those who wish to discern the work of the Spirit in the contemporary cultural context, metaphor can build a bridge across which communication can begin. As we noted in the previous reflection, a metaphor of distinguished pedigree which is reemerging in the Joshua generation to articulate current spiritual sensibility is the metaphor of the monk. Quite by accident I learned the power of this metaphor during a vacation a few years ago. While traveling or waiting to meet friends over this vacation, I would take from my bag a copy of the highly popular book *The Monk who Sold His Ferrari: A Fable about Fulfilling Your Dreams and Reaching Your Destiny,*[10] by Robert Sharma. My attention had been drawn to the book by the large numbers who signed up for a seminar by the author in Dublin in March 2008. The book tells the fictional story of a man called Julian Mantle. He is an invincible lawyer in the courtroom, but taking hold of his own personal life is defeating him. His various addictions eventually lead him to having an almost fatal heart attack in a packed courtroom. His physical collapse brings on a spiritual crisis that forces him to confront the condition of his life and to ask deeper questions about the ultimate meaning of becoming wealthier and more

9. Bandler and Grinder, *The Structure of Magic.*
10. Sharma, *The Monk who Sold His Ferrari.*

famous. Hoping to find answers to his new questions, he embarks upon an eventful journey in India, where he meets some spiritual guides who help him learn how to live with gratitude for the small gifts of every day. The tale presents, in a modern form, the gospel invitation to "Consider the lilies of the field, how they grow; they neither toil nor spin, yet even Solomon in all his glory was not clothed like one of these" (Matt 6:28–29). As I sat in various places reading this book, I was frequently approached by men and women in their twenties and thirties who wanted to start a conversation because they too had read the book and they were interested in discussing the lessons that the main character had learned over the course of the story.

These developments in the metaphorical significance of the monk icon resonate with some themes in recent Catholic writings. The "universal call to holiness" was a particularly special insight of the Second Vatican Council; it is taken up expressly in chapter 5 of the document *Lumen Gentium* (1964), the dogmatic constitution on the church. In spite of the teachings and examples of many great lay saints, it was still commonplace in the early twentieth century to consider holiness the exclusive domain of those in religious life.

Also, the Second Vatican Council document *Ad Gentes*[11] (1965), which is a decree on the missionary activity of the Catholic Church, encouraged those in the established forms of life focused on the spiritual journey—consecrated life groups—to look outwards and to engage with the ascetical and contemplative practices of lifelong practitioners (monks) in the great religious traditions of the world, and to "reflect attentively on how Christian religious life might be able to assimilate the ascetic and contemplative traditions, whose seeds were sometimes planted by God in ancient cultures."[12]

Fourteen years later (26 September 1979) Pope John Paul II, in an address to a delegation of representatives of the traditional schools of Buddhism in Japan,[13] showed a particular concern for cultivating understanding across and between religious traditions in a monastic context: "I congratulate those among you who have lived in small groups in the great Christian monasteries and have shared fully their life of prayer and work for three weeks. Your experience is truly an epoch-making event in

11. *Ad gentes* was promulgated by Pope Paul VI on December 7, 1965.

12. Paul VI, *Ad gentes*, §18.

13. See http://www.fjp2.com/us/john-paul-ii/online-library/audiences/4080 -general-audience-september-26–1979.

the history of inter-religious dialogue." Through such interfaith spiritual dialogues the hope is that a shared spiritual literacy and a shared spiritual vision will be nurtured. Then, drawing on the living spiritual practices of the world's religions, movements such as the new monasticism will contribute to a deep, compassionate prophetic engagement with the great suffering that many people endure today.

Seven years later, on 27 October 1986 John Paul II's unique address to the representatives of the Christian Churches and ecclesial communities and of the world religions in Assisi highlighted how it was historical expressions of the monk archetype—Francis and Clare—that acted as shining lights of the gift of monasticism for today.[14]

> May this holy man and this holy woman inspire all people today to have the same strength of character and love of God and neighbour to continue on the path we must walk together. Moved by the example of Saint Francis and Saint Clare . . . we commit ourselves to re-examine our consciences, to hear its voice more faithfully, to purify our spirits from prejudice, anger, enmity, jealousy and envy. We will seek to be peacemakers in thought and deed, with mind and heart fixed on the unity of the human family.

In the light of the developments outlined above,[15] it makes sense that in his Apostolic Letter on the occasion of the arrival of the new millennium, *Novo millennio ineunte,* Pope John Paul II attached particular importance to another element of monasticism—its opening up of a space within society for like-hearted spiritual seekers. Monasticism supports companionship in the spiritual journey and operates within the horizon of a "spirituality of communion," that is a spirituality of closeness, "being with," "being amidst" others on the journey into God: "To make the Christian community the home and the school of communion: that is the great challenge facing us in the millennium which is now beginning, if we wish to be faithful to the Jesus of the Gospels and respond to the world's deepest yearnings" (paragraph 43).

---

14. See http://www.santegidio.org/it/ecumenismo/uer/1986/papa.htm/.

15. In creating this outline I am indebted to the thesis of John Francis Duggan titled "Multi-religious Experience and Pluralist Attitude: Raimon Panikkar and His Critics" submitted to the Faculty of Theology of Regis College and the Theology Department of the Toronto School of Theology in partial fulfillment of the requirements for the degree of Doctor of Philosophy in Theology and awarded by the University of St. Michael's College in 2000.

He went on to explain that this spirituality of communion is grounded in contemplative appreciation of the spiritual journey that Jesus himself had steadfastly followed: "Let us have no illusions: unless we follow this spiritual path" lived by Jesus, "external structures of communion will serve very little purpose. They would become mechanisms without a soul, 'masks' of communion rather than its means of expression and growth."[16]

A deeper appreciation of Jesus's own spiritual journey has come to the fore as a central theme in contemporary monastic/contemplative authors. The Augustinian contemplative teacher Martin Laird has helpfully presented the historical precedents for this appreciation. He has highlighted how the fourth-century Christian teacher Evagrius, in line with the contemplative school in which he practiced, interpreted the temptation of Jesus in the desert, not as abstract teaching about power and lust, but as a teaching about the use of short Scripture phrases "in order to break the cycle of inner chatter that would only hold his attention captive the more he listened to it and indulged it."[17] Cynthia Bourgeault highlights the same theme in contemporary Christian spirituality in the West by employing the term "Wisdom Jesus." Thus she invites her readers to approach the Gospels with a view to learning how to live with the Wisdom of Jesus so as to put on his mind (Phil 2:5); our call as Christians is not to "just admiring Jesus, but acquiring his consciousness."[18] Bourgeault in turn has been influenced by the Camaldolese monk Bruno Barnhart, whom she describes as "one of my most important mentors." Barnhart has asserted that "Western Christianity has given less attention to the revolution in consciousness than to the affective and moral conversions"[19] which an encounter with Christ initiates.

Contemporary theologians have also provided a multitude of insights into the emergent monastic/contemplative turn of the West. The eminent late German Jesuit theologian Karl Rahner has highlighted the struggle in recent spiritual practitioners to reintegrate mysticism and prophetic action. In his 1963 book *Visions and Prophecies* Rahner notes:

> it can be said with but little exaggeration that the history of mystical theology is a history of the devaluation of the prophetic

16. Pope John Paul II, *Novo Millennio Ineunte*, paragraph 43.

17. Laird, *A Sunlit Absence*, 13.

18. Bourgeault, *The Wisdom Jesus*, 29.

19. Barnhart, *Second Simplicity*, 51. See also, Barnhart, *The Future of Wisdom*.

element in favour of non-prophetic, "pure", infused contemplation . . . Nevertheless prophecy has its foundation in Scripture,
and in practice a great history in the Church . . . yet orthodox
theology (which I note includes spirituality) has never paid any
serious attention to the question of whether there are prophets
even in post-apostolic times, how their spirit can be recognized
and discerned . . . what the import of their mission for the exterior and inner life of the church.[20]

The late German woman theologian Dorothee Soelle made Rahner's
insight more concrete when she defined mysticism not as a new vision
of God but as a different relationship with the world—one that has borrowed the eyes of God.[21] A quick visit to the Women's Rights section of
the Human Rights Watch[22] website will reveal that the eyes of God still
need to be cast today on the breadth and depth of women's oppression
across the globe, which extends from poverty and domestic abuse to sex
slavery. The majority of the world's poor are women. Female babies are
more at risk than male babies of violent attack. Double standards in sexual matters affect women in harmful ways in all cultures and economic
groups across the globe. In the shadow of these realities it is an ethical
requirement that all today who study, teach, or live mysticism do so in the
context of the desolate, inconsolable grief of the women who are brutal-
ized by rape, famine, and child death on a daily basis. Women who have
embraced solitude throughout history, and today, have always tended to
carry in their hearts and have struggled for the relief of gender-based
suffering.

Sarah Coakley has been a strong contemporary advocate of the
power of a commitment to nurturing contemplative attentiveness for
activating social compassion: "The moral and epistemic stripping that is
endemic to the act of contemplation is a vital key here: its practical self-
emptying inculcates an attentiveness that is beyond merely good political intentions. Its practice is more discomforting, more destabilizing to
settled presumptions, than a simple *design* on empathy."[23]

Matthew Eggemeier has observed that Coakley's assertion of the
sociopolitical fall-out from the cultivation of contemplative attentiveness

20. Rahner, *Visions and Prophecies*, 20–21.

21. Soelle, *The Silent Cry*, 292–93.

22 See http://www.hrw.org/women/.

23. Coakley, "Is There a Future for Gender and Theology?" 2–12, quotation on 6–7.

reflects a strong influence from Simone Weil.[24] For Weil the self could most effectively be dispossessed of its insular focus by entering into the practice of opening to God in contemplative attentiveness. In opening to God, the self is decentered in a manner that prepares it for decentering in the context of the suffering of the world, in whatever form this presents itself.[25] Similarly Etty Hillesum, who like Weil was a victim of the Holocaust, embraced the practice of solitude so as to expand the space within herself to receive and transform the suffering of the world in which she was immersed: "There is always a quiet room in some corner of our being, and we can always retire there for a while. Surely they can't rob us of that. For a whole year now I have been working at that quiet space within me, so that it has now expanded into a great hall, palpably present."[26]

Contemporary reflection on the relationship between contemplation and compassion has also turned to great classical mystical resources such as John of the Cross's account of the dark nights, which provides an enduring image of soul pain which can be induced in people's lives in the face of innocent suffering. The Carmelite writer Constance Fitzgerald has been particularly insightful in this regard. As she has indicated in her seminal essay on the theme of "Impasse and the Dark Night,"[27] it is not her intention to apply a Christian theme (i.e., the dark night) to a contemporary issue (i.e., the violation of women's rights); rather she has attempted to understand whether the dark night may have new forms today, particularly in the struggle of women today for a more just and wholesome experience of life in our world. Beverly Lanzetta, a feminist new monastic who shares her personal expression of the theme of this book in the epilogue, has vividly described what is happening in the lives of women who contemplatively engage the impasse generated by their encounters with gender-based violence or discrimination.[28] When the real suffering of women, the disabled, and majority-world citizens (to name but a few groups) passes through contemplative appropriation the result will not be passive resignation. The questioning, and restlessness of

24. Eggemeier, "A Mysticism of Open Eyes," 43–62, quotation on 55.

25. Weil, *Waiting for God.*

26. Hillesum, *Etty,* 473–74. An insightful overview of Ettys's spirituality may be found in Maas, "Etty Hllesum: 'In me is the Earth and in me is Heaven,'" in Maas, *Spirituality as Insight,* 112–45.

27. FitzGerald, "Impasse and the Dark Night," in J. Wolski-Conn, *Women's Spirituality,* 410–50.

28. Lanzetta, *Radical Wisdom,* 73–77.

the contemplative stance of the new monastic is generating explorations at the frontiers of *faith seeking understanding and transformation.*

As the Vatican II *Pastoral Constitution on the Church in the Modern World* reminded its readers and hearers, "the joys and hopes, the grief and anguish of people today, especially those who are poor or afflicted in any way are the joys and hopes the grief and anguish of those live in the spirit of Jesus" (paragraph 1). Nothing genuinely fails to move the hearts of today's Christian new monastics. Ultimately, the call to discern spiritual experience in Western society today is the call to develop the heart and mind of a poet. We live in a world of unpredictable change, diversity, and new times. We cannot pin the action of the Spirit to stable anchors in such a sea of change. Instead, as Schelling posits, "the objective world is the original, yet unconscious, poetry of the spirit."[29] Attunement to contemporary spiritual experience calls us to attentiveness, not to "look *for* something, but to dwell *in* this world by letting it be as it is."[30]

Those who are actively involved in reading the shape and contours of contemporary spirituality find themselves drawn into a self-implicating exploration that requires the virtues of those who take up spiritual disciplines.[31] These virtues include the capacity to be radically attentive to the still small voice of mystery as it is spoken in reflective conversations with spiritual seekers, and the willingness to set aside one's familiar maps of the spiritual journey in order to go on pilgrimage in new territories of the soul.

Attunement to contemporary spiritual experience calls for attentiveness, to avoid imposing familiar melodies on the Spirit's new rhythm, to learn the new dance, which has the flexibility capable of moving in motion with a pneumatological outpouring. There is much to learn from women who have lived such innovative adaptability through the ages, as we shall see in the next six chapters.

Questions for Reflection / Journaling

- What are your observations about the spiritual quest in the West today?

29. Schelling, *Samtliche Werke*, 3:349, quoted in translation in Burrows, "Raiding the Inarticulate," 173–94; quotation on 185.

30. Ibid.

31. Frohlich, "Spiritual Discipline, Discipline of Spirituality," 65–78.

- Have you been challenged by the spiriutality and self-help sections of bookshops that you visit?

- What groups, advertisements, gatherings, and publications capture for you the spirit of the contemporary spiritual quest in the West?

- Have you reflected on the spiritual practice of Jesus? What have you learned from your reflection?

- Who has inspired you among contemporary mystic prophets?

- In your own journaling what are the metaphors distinctive to your vision of the spiritual journey?

Narratives of Solitude Fulfilled

1

Syncletica

Embracing Solitude in Early African Christianity[1]

PROFOUND CHANGES IN THE spiritual culture of a historical era are often extroverted into the landscape. These spiritual changes are usually grounded in shifts in social, political, and economic realities. The latter realities were particularly important in the birth of the early Christian embrace of solitude in the North African desert. While some historians have linked the rise of Egyptian desert anchorites with *ananchoresis*—the term used in fourth-century Egypt to describe the phenomenon of tax evasion by means of flight—this etymology is not widely accepted.[2] Instead, the spiritual movements of committed Christians seeking solitude who migrated to secluded settings on the urban margins or in the desert were mainly constituted of persons who enjoyed the benefits of the rising wealth of cities. The widely acknowledged founder of the north African exodus-to-the-desert movement, St Antony of Egypt (252–356), was reputed to have had a considerable amount of land. This affluence was not sufficient, however, to satisfy the deeper yearnings of Antony and many others like him, and a city with an alternative culture grew from the migration of these seekers to the desert.

Peter Brown, in his classic work on sexual renunciation in early Christianity, describes well the iconic character of the move to the desert.[3] Moving out to the uninhabited place set the desert dwellers apart

1. A less developed version of the material below may be found in Flanagan, "Visionary Women: From Past Icons to Future Inspiration," in Howells and Tyler, *Sources of Transformation*, 73–92. Copyright permission granted.

2. Rubenson, *The Letters of St Antony*, 116.

3. Brown, *The Body and Society*, 214.

from the busy life of urban Christians. The journey to the secluded place enacted the process of disengagement from the dominant expression of Christian community at that time. The strangeness and challenges of the new landscape are captured in the variety of insects and other intimidating creatures that inhabit the writings of the desert solitaries. These insects may be considered as archetypal representations of the manner in which the radical change of external geography, achieved in the move to the desert, evoked new spiritual awareness in its thoughtful inhabitants. The routines of the city, set by common work patterns and shared city services, had melted. A new sense of being at home in this strange land had to be cultivated. Foundations had to be set in a place where no roots had yet been sent forth. The confirmation of vocation had to be wrenched from an unflinching engagement with the environment and fanned into sustainability by daily attention. The dwelling chosen had to create the conditions for the dweller to step back from immersion in daily trivialities and yet provide the dweller with perspective on the surrounding rhythms of life.[4] Drawing closer to one of those who took this journey into the desert may illuminate women's new search today for solitude.

Amma Syncletica (270–350 CE)[5]

It has first to be acknowledged that the historical factuality of Syncletica has been contested, so in referring to her life and work I will build on the scholarship of Kevin Corrigan, who has made a strong scholarly case for accepting the reality of her life and contribution to the early Church.[6] The text of her life was little known until the seventeenth century when there was a general revival of interest in early Christian literature. In the West a tradition developed in the fourteenth century of attributing the authorship of her life to Athanasius[7] and of designating Syncletica as the

---

4. Lane, *Fierce Landscapes*, 163.

5. Swan, *The Forgotten Desert Mothers*, 41–63.

6. Corrigan, "Syncletica and Macrina," 241–57. Kevin has served as dean (1991–1998) and as director of the Classical, Mediaeval, and Renaissance Studies Program St. Thomas More College, University of Saskatchewan, Canada.

7. The Life of Syncletica is preserved in Syriac and has been falsely attributed to Athanasius of Alexandria (d. 373). It is most likely that is a translation of a Greek original composed between the fifth and ninth centuries.

foundress of female monasticism, paralleling Antony as the founder of male monasticism.[8]

Given the focus here on Syncletica, there is then the further challenge of choosing an approach to reading her life and teaching in a manner that illuminates the contemporary emergence of new monasticism. Mary Schaffer's study of the text of the *Life of Syncletica* provides an excellent scholarly account of the form and structure of the text, as well as the influences evident in it from surrounding theological, biblical, and spiritual writers and teachers. Schaffer attributes her original insights into the text to her practice of "contemplative" engagement with the text. Similarly here, the text has been read with a contemplative attentiveness to the teaching it can offer to women embracing a spirituality of solitude today.

I do not intend to get involved in the sociocultural meaning of the ascetic behavior of women in the ancient Greco-Roman world. Instead, I accept the work of a wide community of scholars that has argued that the solitary, celibate choice of women in this era was not a private religious choice but an embodied protest against the social roles to which women were assigned.[9] Lastly, I will read the available fragmentary material in the awareness that while the textual sources are limited, the overall conclusion of contemporary scholarship is that in this era "women's asceticism had sizable numbers, varied lifestyles and considerable vigor."[10] At all times the originality of the imagery in the text witnesses to a vivid personal voice behind the author's inscriptions.[11]

Amma Syncletica grew up in the city of Alexandria in Egypt. She was rich, well educated, and interested in spiritual questions from early in her life. She resisted her parents' encouragement to get married. After the death of her parents, she sold all that she had, distributed the funds to the poor, and moved from her parents' home, with her blind sister, to the vicinity of the family tomb on the outskirts of the city.[12] Just as the

8. A discussion of the transmission of the Life of Syncletica is available in Schaffer, *The Life & Regimen of the Blessed & Holy Syncletica*, 31–32.

9. Wimbush, *Ascetic Behavior in Greco-Roman Antiquity*, 8.

10. Harmless, *Desert Christians*, 440–45.

11. Studies helpful in reading Syncletica today, apart from those mentioned in the notes above, are Castelli, "Mortifying the Body," 134–53; Forman, "Amma Syncletica," 199–237.

12. Tombs at the edge of the city were also the location for Antony of Egypt's spiritual journey. Goehring, "The Encroaching Desert," 281–96 explores how such spaces

teaching of many other solitaries of the fourth century is still available to us today, so the wisdom of Amma Syncletica is recorded in the collection of aphorisms which in Greek is called *Apophthegmata*.[13] In this collection of brief wisdom teachings from 127 "desert fathers," she is one of only three women, the other two being Amma Theodora and Amma Sarah.[14] She is credited with twenty-seven sayings in this collection. Further information regarding her life and spirituality is available in a fifth-century document by Pseudo-Athanasius, *The Life & Regimen of the Blessed and Holy Teacher Syncletica*.[15]

As previously stated, the purpose here is to reflect on perennial aspects of the life of this fourth-century woman spiritual innovator against the background of the increasing number of women who set out on a God quest by embracing forms of intentional solitude today.[16] In this context, what is immediately striking is the dialectic between Syncletica authoring the shape and style of her own committed spiritual journey, while at the same time her journey enriches and builds up the Christian community around her. It is also notable how she was reluctant to assume the spiritual leadership thrust on her as she wrestled with the uncertainties generated by moving in an uncharted path. In Saying Nine from the *Apophthegmata* she communicates vividly in the imagery of sailing[17] the uncertainty and struggles that were the atmosphere of her journey:

> Those of us who put out to sea at first sail with a favorable wind; then the sails spread, but later the winds become adverse. Then the ship is tossed by the waves and is no longer controlled by the rudder. But when in a little while there is calm, and the tempest dies down, then the ship sails on again. So it is with us.

---

are the literary artifacts of solitude.

13. Ward, *The Sayings of the Desert Fathers: The Alphabetical Collection*, 193–97.

14. Margot King has done exceptional work in locating over a thousand named Desert Mothers. See http://www.peregrina.com/matrologia_latina/DesertMothers1 .html/.

15. Pseudo-Athanasius, *The Life & Regimen of the Blessed & Holy Teacher Syncletica*. Interpretative assistance is available in Schaffer, *The Life & Regimen of the Blessed & Holy Syncletica*. See also. Forman, *Praying with the Desert Mothers*, 47–58.

16. There has been a recent explosion of interest in the wisdom of the Desert Mothers as evident in the expanding collection of publications: Earle, *The Desert Mothers: Prayer*; Earle, *The Desert Mothers: Spiritual Practices*; Chryssavgis, *In the Heart of the Desert*; Keller, *Oasis of Wisdom*; Bagin, *Metericon*.

17. Paragraphs 19 and 47 of *The Life* are also replete with sailing imagery.

It would be easy today to look back on this era of innovation in the form of the God quest among women and imagine that those living in those early Christian centuries could see the same patterns that we can observe with the benefits of hindsight and historical analysis. Indeed the imagery of the sea conveys how much Syncletica's quest was carried along by a power much greater than her personal inner resources, a power that is intuitively learned rather than read from a map in unerring detail.

Amid the confusion about the core identity of the Christian community that overshadowed these times (because the persecution of Christians had gone into decline), the anchoritic asceticism explosion, exhibited in the life of Syncetica, broke forth. As James Goehring has clearly argued in his account of the origins of monasticism,

> it was the spirit of the times and the new Christian faith that produced the explosion, and as it welled forth from below, it burst onto the plane of history independently throughout the empire. One may still discover influences on specific forms of asceticism and trace various pathways of development, but the quest for the "origins" of Christian monasticism should be let go.[18]

Syncletica was attuned to this imperceptible development. This intuitive capacity resembles in some ways the instinct a small number of animals displayed on 26 December 2004, causing them to flee territory where a tsunami would later wreak devastation.[19] Two features of authentic religious innovation emerge here. First, those at the forefront are attuned to the deepest soul movements in their society and have the courage to create a response to the insight they intuit. Second, many such innovators will arise simultaneously, without structured collaboration. It is as a witness to such patterns that Syncletica contributes to the reflection on the meaning of the emergence of solitude-embracing forms of life among women today.

When the originating inspiration of Syncletica's life choice is investigated further, we find that the incipient impulse for the journey displays a love-mysticism[20] character. While she displays solidarity with those in need through her disbursement of the proceeds of the sale of her inheritance, material service of the needy is not the core expression of her

18. Goehring, *Ascetics, Society and the Desert*, 35.

19. Kaplan, "When Animals Predict Earthquakes."

20. Ruffing, "Encountering Love Mysticism," 20–33.

personal vocation. Instead, the account of her life reveals that the core experience of her life that she sought to share with others was the experience of a passionate love affair between God and her. In paragraph 92 of her *Life* she turns to marriage as the metaphor for explaining to those who sought her counsel the journey she was undertaking: "The spectacle of a secular marriage should be a model for us." The text continues to paint a sensuous image of the love relationship to which her hearers are invited to dispose themselves. For Syncletica, the person in love with God ought to recall the sweetness of perfumes, the texture of fine clothes, and the glitter of the jewelry of the brides in the surrounding society. These images, in her view, evoke the beauty of divine intimacy. Only a radically embodied love is a worthy energy for a life commitment to the Divine. All actions and good deeds must flow from the commitment made in and through love, "for our beloved will not at all receive us hospitably unless he receives our promises."

Pseudo-Athanasius shows how Syncletica believed that her personal vocation to spiritual guidance arose primarily from God's desire for her to speak of her loving relationship to others:

> God knows how to proclaim by himself those who love him toward the correcting of those who hear. Then therefore some began to enter with a desire for that which is better and to make entreaties for their own edification. For they approached the ways she led her life, wishing to be helped and according to the accustomed formula asked her, "in what way is it necessary to be saved?"[21]

In a similar manner Syncletica encourages those she guides to give space and time for God to do God's work and for the relationship with God to "hatch." This relationship has its own dynamic and the ability to allow that dynamic to take its course is foundational to discovering what God is doing. She realizes that it can be more attractive to move around from one new development to the next rather than to settle into the rhythm of the journey God is calling to be undertaken. In Saying 6 she advises: "If you find yourself in a monastery do not go to another place, for that will harm you a great deal. Just as the bird who abandons the eggs she was sitting on prevents them from hatching, so the monk or the nun grows cold and their faith dies, when they go from one place to another."

21. *The Life*, par. 21.

In all her words of guidance available to us today, what is particularly remarkable is the freshness and clarity of her language. Prophetic teachers in every age have been set apart by their innovative use of symbols and metaphors, and this is true also for Syncletica. In her First Saying from the *Apophthegmata* the parallel she draws between the challenges of drawing near to God and the struggle to make a fire from scratch is deeply evocative:

> For those who are making their way to God there is at first great struggle and effort, but then indescribable joy. For just as those who wish to kindle a fire are at first choked with smoke, suffer watery eyes, and in this way achieve their purpose . . . so we too must kindle the divine fire within us with tears and effort.[22]

Another image in paragraph 93 of her *Life* innovatively illustrates the single mindedness with which she cultivated sensitive spiritual awareness. It takes up the classical theme of the need to make choices for the sake of fully responding to God's drawing; thus one cannot serve two masters simultaneously. Syncletica depicts this enduring teaching through the image of drawing water from the well. "Just as it is not possible to bring up at the same time two buckets filled with water since, by the turning of the windlass, the one bucket is lowered empty and the other is brought up full, so it is in our case."[23]

In the values and commitments described above, Syncletica is not some exotic specimen of an archaic, idiosyncratic spiritual practitioner. What she does, she does on behalf of humanity. The journey she travels in freely taking up an unmapped form of spiritual commitment enables her to counsel wisely those who wish to bring the same integrity of spirit to their own life circumstances in diverse settings. She asserts that it would be "dangerous" for anyone to attempt to guide others on a journey that has not been personally undertaken. The journey into solitude is a necessary preparation for the authentic spiritual guide and teacher.

> It is dangerous for someone not "formed" by experience of the ascetic life to try to teach; it is as if someone whose house is unsound were to receive guests and cause them injury by the collapse of the building. In the same way these people also destroy along with themselves those who have come to them, by not first building securely their own way of life . . . For the mere

22. Ibid., par. 60.
23. Ibid., par. 93.

articulation of words is like inscriptions painted in perishable colours which a very short period of time has destroyed with blasts of wind and splashes of rain. Teaching that is based on ascetic experience, on the other hand, not even all eternity could destroy.[24]

Authentic spiritual guides must also have gained fluency in the spiritual language of the era in which they live. Informed by the spiritual maps of her times, Syncletica draws on the concept of *logismoi* in order to communicate effectively with her hearers. This concept, which was formalized into eight dimensions by Evagrius of Pontus[25] (346–399), provides an analytical tool for explaining various manifestations of human resistance, struggle, and avoidance of the call to live with an alert and compassionate humanity. While the *logismoi* schema subsequently mutated into the "seven deadly sins," in its original form it provided a useful diagnostic structure for those offering spiritual guidance. In the *logismoi* schema the daily practices regarding food, possessions, emotional states, and relationships were recognized as the warp and woof of one's commitments to spiritual integrity. Syncletica's guidance on managing anger and resentment ("remembrance of wrongs") displays her skills of communication as a teacher and her deep psychological understanding:

> Anger, like smoke, disappears once it has disturbed the soul for a while, but remembrance of wrongs, as if embedded in the soul, renders it more formidable than a wild beast. Even a dog, enraged against someone, relinquishes its anger when coaxed with tidbit; and the other beast also becomes gentle with habit. One who is governed by remembrance of wrongs, however, is not persuaded by entreaty, nor made gentle by food, nor indeed does time that transforms all things heal the suffering of such a person.[26]

Syncletica's personifications of anger and resentment make her teaching vivid and dramatic, and caused her teaching to be remembered more readily than if it had been delivered in a more abstract way. In solitude she had confronted the vagaries of the human heart, and she brought the richness of this experience to her ministry of spiritual companionship.

24. Ibid., par. 79.

25. Evagrius, *The Praktikos, Chapters on Prayer*, 16–20: gluttony (§7), impurity (§8), avarice (§9), sadness (§10), anger (§11), acedia (§12), vainglory (§13), and pride (§14).

26. *The Life*, par. 63.

In her direct immersion in the society of her day, unprotected by husband, brother, or father, Syncletica developed acute sensitivity to the unique challenges women faced in any attempt to live authentically. She put the truth before her female hearers that "towards women generally there is a great hostility in the world"[27] and so invited honesty from them regarding the circumstances of their lives. She also challenged them regarding their support for each other as women. She reminded them that there can be a strong temptation for women to be jealous of those women who may appear to have more successful lives. Whether women follow the accepted social path or resist it, it is important for Syncletica that solidarity is maintained: "For in giving birth women die in labour; and yet in failing to give birth, they waste away under reproaches that they are barren and unfruitful."[28] She also invites honesty regarding the intimate relationships of the lives of her hearers. Has lesbianism been an aspect of their experience? she asks; or how intimate have they become to male spiritual advisors in their lives? she inquires.[29] She was a woman who initiated the most intimately honest conversations with those she guided, knowing that the truth would set them free.

Through the inclusion of her sayings in the *Apophthegmata*, Syncletica's wisdom was translated into Latin in the sixth century and so has remained available in the Western spiritual tradition. The sayings were taken up in the anchoritic tradition in the past, such as the thirteenth-century English spiritual classic *Ancrene Wisse* (a guide for anchoresses).[30] It may be no accident that in the 1990s her life (i.e., her biography) became available in a modern English translation for the first time with the emergence of new intentional forms of spiritual communities. Embracing the values of solitude may provide a new occasion to access the overflow of meaning in this classical text. From the text we see that Syncletica's embrace of solitude bore fruit:

- in a creative capacity to speak a new religious language in her society

- in an ability to offer wise counsel from the garden of solitude where deep knowledge of the human spirit had been harvested

- in a power to attract others to gospel living

27. Ibid., 42.

28. Ibid.

29. Ibid., par. 27.

30. *Anchoritic Spirituality*, 41–208. Syncletica is mentioned on pp. 50 and 108.

Her life was a generative commitment to a new way that went forward in the lives of those who became her companions in the journey.

The Desert and the Future

Today theologians such as Stanley Hauerwas are reimaging the impulse that drove the desert solitaries. Attention is being drawn to the need to step out of the stable patterns of the religious world as it has been known in modernity if today's new cultural context is to be engaged. This is a time when a life commitment to contemplative practice can expect to embrace radical change. Stanley Hauerwas is a representative of the neo-orthodox response to modernity. He has been consistently critical of most forms of expression of Christian concern by the churches and argues for a radical discontinuity between Christianity and any given culture. His argument is that theology (and spirituality) since the Enlightenment have tended to ask the wrong question—how to make the gospel credible in the modern world. Instead he asserts that the Christian faith is an invitation to be part of what he terms an "alien people."[31] A constant call echoes through his writings for the church to renew itself as a distinctive community. He is also unhappy that Christian politics has come to mean Christian social activism: "much of what passes for Christian social concern today, of the left or right, is the social concern of a Church that seems to have despaired of being Church."[32] It follows from his argument then that the challenge for intentional spiritual communities in the present cultural climate is the development of a way of life in which the mystical character of vocation is central.

It should come as no surprise that the life of a woman in the North African desert in the fourth century should provide a mirror reflecting the monastic-like search for solitude amongst women today back onto itself. The legacy of these desert spiritual innovators has provided inspiration to countless new spiritual movements through the centuries and has been a frequent reference point for many developments in contemporary

31. Hauerwas and Willimon, *Resident Aliens*, 30. The theme of assuming a certain distance from contemporary culture is also evident in the writings of Lesslie Newbigin. With a background of years of experience in cross-cultural missionary engagement with Hinduism in India, Newbigin was acutely aware of the need to develop a degree of distance from Enlightenment-driven society to engage in a similar cross-cultural missionary task. Newbigin, *The Gospel in a Pluralist Society*.

32. Hauerwas, *A Community of Character*, 80.

spirituality.[33] Religious innovators like Charles de Foucault and new monastic expressions like the Monastic Fraternities of Jerusalem spring to mind as examples of those who find inspiration in the desert for our times. Reading Syncletica's life (i.e., biography) from the experience of emergent new forms of embracing solitude among women may reveal some of the deeper movements at work in this development.

33. Nouwen, *The Way of the Heart*; Jones, *Soul Making*; Christie, *The Word in the Desert*; Belisle, *The Language of Silence*.

2

Moninne

Embracing Solitude in Irish/Celtic Christianity[1]

IRISH MONASTICISM FROM ITS earliest expressions was inspired by the desire to imitate the spiritual journeys undertaken in the desert of Egypt. The *Antiphonary of Bangor*, an ancient Latin manuscript associated with the early Irish abbey of Bangor in Northern Ireland, and which was written between 680 and 691, contains nineteen references to Egypt. The quatrain below extolling Irish monasticism is typical of such references:

> A House full of Delights
>
> Built on Rock
>
> A veritable vine
>
> Transmitted from Egypt.[2]

The connection with Egyptian solitude movements was also carved into the stone memoirs—the high crosses—of the Irish monastic movement. Both high crosses on the ninth-century monastic site of Castledermot, in the east of Ireland, have depictions of Antony of Egypt.

Immersion in a desert-like solitude was the bedrock from which the first expressions of the early Irish monastic tradition emerged. In their enthusiastic identification with the Egyptian precedent early Irish

---

1. A less developed version of the material below may be found in Flanagan, "Visionary Women," in Howells and Tyler, *Sources of Transformation*, 73–92.

2. For the text see Warren, *The Antiphonary of Bangor*, 2:28.
Domus deliciis plena
Super petram constructa
Necon vinea vera
Ex Aegypto transducta

monastics chose hermitages and small eremitic colonies to pursue their God quest. The isolated desert quality of the chosen locations in the Irish countryside for these old hermitages is still recognizable by the presence of words like *dysert* or *disert* in contemporary place names. Thus the aforementioned monastery in Castledermot, which was founded by Dermot is known locally as *Dísert Diarmada* (the desert of Dermot), the good quality of the local agricultural land notwithstanding.[3] More determined solitaries, however, sought their desert on islands off the coast.[4]

As in Egypt, so in Ireland women as well as men forged singular paths of spiritual innovation, though as was also the case in Egypt, the female trajectory is harder to trace. Research has shown, for example, how in an early life of Brigit of Kildare a story is told of about a religious woman who lived on her own and did not have adequate resources to create a meal of welcome for a visit from Brigit that would do justice to Brigit's social stature. When this story from her life was being redacted in a twelfth-century account of Brigit's life, the woman receiving Brigit was no longer presented on her own but as living with a small group of women.[5] In a similar way, we find that the while primary Irish women saints are noted by name and individually for their religious innovation, there tends to be a focus on the later phases of their lives when surrounded by companions, rather than on the earlier, solitary stage as religious innovators. There is a further limitation imposed in reading a woman's life from this era as a resource for understanding the contemporary emergence of new monasticism. As the Cambridge historian Kathleen Hughes has noted, the lives of women religious innovators from this era have never been adequately studied. Thus while "119 Irish women or groups of women are celebrated in the Martyrology of Tallaght (and all November and part of December is missing) . . . we have lives of only four women saints, Brigit of Kildare (d. 517/9), Samthann of Clonbroney(d. 524/6), Íte of Killeedy (d. 570/7), and Darerca/Monenna of Killeevy (d. 518)."[6]

In a more general reflection on the legacy of this period in Irish religious history, Kathleen Hughes and Ann Hamlin have noted that "when

---

3. De Bhaldraithe, "The Three Orders of Irish Saints," 58–83; quotation on 67.

4. The *Vita Sancti Columbae* by Adamnan, 167, is full of these references. The following example is typical: "Some of our brethren have lately set sail, and are anxious to discover a desert in the pathless sea." (*Aliqui ex nostris nuper emigraverunt, desertum in pelago intransmeabili invenire optantes*).

5. Harrington, *Women in a Celtic Church*, 124.

6. Hughes, *Early Christian Ireland*, 234.

we think of the Irish church we must think of a monastic church which performed spiritual duties for the laity."[7] The architectural structure of these early monastic communities in Ireland is notable for the space provided for an individual's spiritual journey within a communal spiritual journey. Small dwelling spaces were dispersed in groups throughout the large common shared space of the monastic site. The solitude which such a single dwelling space provided was unknown outside monastic enclosures since "it was colder and more dangerous and a waste of precious space and fuel."[8] Small communal prayer spaces—oratories—were also omnipresent. When monastic settlements grew in size and assumed the character of a town in terms of the diversity of services they supported— teaching, baking, pottery, laundry—the choice was not made to build a large oratory but rather to create several smaller oratories.[9] The symbolic intimacy of a small space bespoke the intimacy of the spiritual journey being undertaken. Those who made this journey the special focus of their lives were not isolated in this call, but encountered the bustle of daily life as they made their way around the monastic space, which in Kildare and other places had a boundary without a wall.[10] The centripetal force that pulled the monastic site together was spiritual leadership provided by a spiritual teacher or the tradition of a saint. We will now attend reflectively to the legacy of one of these early Irish women innovators[11] in order throw light on what those embracing solitude within a social context (whether family, urban complex, or rural village) may be called to.

Darerca/Moninne (c. 432–518)[12]

At the outset it has to be acknowledged that the lives of women from the early Irish Christian era are primarily communicated in a hagiographical

7. Hughes and Hamlin, *The Modern Traveller to the Early Irish Church*, 7.

8. Bitel, *Isle of the Saints*, 79.

9. De Paor and de Paor, *Early Christian Ireland*, 54.

10. Bitel, *Isle of the Saints*, 63.

11. The Irish Cistercian scholar, Eoin de Bhaldraithe has divided the Irish experience of monasticism into three phases of development, similar to those recounted in the *Catalogus Sanctorum Hiberniae secundum diversa tempora*. Moninne lived in the first phase (425–549 CE), which is the only phase that did not reject the ministry and company of women and laity in the monastic enterprise. See article in n. 2 above.

12. The available lives of Moninne / Monenna / Moninna date from the eleventh or early twelfth century. Earlier texts are presumed to be the source of the available lives.

genre. Recent research into this genre of writing has changed the reception of lives wrapped in this narrative tradition. It is no longer considered to be simply a devotional genre, amplifying the holiness of the saint; rather hagiography is now considered to offer a window on the society that produced it.[13] Against this background, University College Dublin scholar Elva Johnston has argued that "Irish hagiography bears the imprint of an aristocratic, clerical and stratified society that circumscribes the roles of women."[14]

What we read then in the lives of early Irish women religious innovators is a socially androcentric perspective on women's new spiritual engagements. Within this perspective two approaches characterize the hagiographies: minimalist reporting of women religious innovators; robust reporting of the negative reception of the new spiritual autonomy claimed by women through frequent accounts of the abduction, rape and murder of virgins; and positive reporting of women who displayed "manly" virtues in their new lives.[15]

From among the early Irish women spiritual innovators I have chosen to investigate the life of Darerca/Moninne because the account of her life is marked by a metaphor that became a significant part of women's spirituality beyond this era and beyond Ireland: "for she had a manly spirit in a woman's body."[16] Through this metaphor, which I will return to later, the capacity for classical overflow of meaning is imprinted in her life. Her life has been transmitted in two versions.[17] The shorter version has been preserved in the medieval collection of saints' lives known as *Codex Salmanticensis*, which is held today in Bibliothèque Royale Albert

---

See Sharpe, *Medieval Irish Saints' Lives*, 396–97.

13. Herbert, "Hagiography," in McCone and Simms, *Progress in Medieval Irish Studies*, 79–90.

14. Johnston, "The 'Pagan' and 'Christian' Identities of Irish Female Saints," in Atherton, *Celts and Christians*, 60–78; quotation on 62.

15. Bitel, "Women's Monastic Enclosures in Early Ireland," 15–36.

16. Sperber, "The Life of St Monenna or Darerca of Killevy," in Hughes and Nolan, *Armagh History and Society*, 63–97; quotation on 74.

17. A thorough discussion of the history of collecting saints' lives can be found in Sharpe, *Medieval Irish Saints' Lives*. The possible origins of *Codex Salmanticensis* in the northern region of Ireland has been discussed by T. M. Charles-Edwards, "The Northern Lectionary: A Source for the *Codex Salmanticensis*?," in Cartwright, *Celtic Hagiography and Saints' Cults*, 148–60.

I in Brussels. The life is believed by scholars to be an abbreviated version of an earlier life.[18]

This earlier life is also believed by scholars to provide the source for the much longer, and somewhat confused, second life by Conchubranus that can be found in the seventeenth-century collection of saints' lives edited by Mario Espositio and known as *Vitae Sanctorum Hiberniae*.[19] This second life dates back to the eleventh century when Conchubranus rewrote the earlier life of Moninna in a longer version and created a narrative of the saint traveling (on a floating island) to Scotland and England to found monasteries, including a church on Andresey. Burton Abbey, which was founded in 1004, had no saint's cult of its own so the monks adopted nearby Modwenna of Andresey, an island in the river Trent adjacent to the town of Burton upon Trent. When in 1114 Geoffrey became abbot of Burton, he developed a strong devotion to the cult of Modwenna and made inquiries in Ireland for material about her. Eventually a copy of Conchubranus's *Life* arrived at Burton. He found the information unsatisfactory, and he therefore decided to rewrite it. The main changes Geoffrey made were to add more details about Modwenna's Anglo-Saxon associates.

Scholarly opinion suggests that the early life behind *Codex Salmanticensis* and Conchubranus's text "was probably written in the first quarter of the seventh century under the patronage of her fourth successor as abbess of Killevy."[20] In the analysis below I will draw on the *Codex Salmanticensis* version of the life.

While Darerca was the birth name of the woman whose life I am reading against the horizon of the reemergence of intentional solitude practices among women today, Moninne was her acquired name.[21] She was born into a family that ruled the territory stretching from Louth to Armagh. Tradition held that Saint Patrick visited her home and baptized her when she was born, giving her the name of his own sister, Darerca. Several themes weave their way through her life. A distinct element emphasized in the account of her life is the love of learning that fills her life from her childhood. This love of learning is communicated through

18. Translation by Ingrid Sperber. See n. 16, above.

19. *The Life*, 63.

20. Callan, "St. Darerca and Her Sister Scholars," 32–49; quotation on 44.

21. It was common in early Irish hagiography for saints to have different names at different stages of life: P. Russell, "Patterns of Hypcorism in Early Irish Hagiography," in Carey et al., *Studies in Irish Hagiography*, 237–49.

the narrative of the diverse teachers which were part of her life, many
of whom were intentionally sought out by her. In the beginning she was
mentored by a local priest, where "she made great progress in a short
time."[22] Local opportunities for more advanced study were limited and
so later she moved to the western seaboard with some companions to be
mentored by bishop Ibar of the Aran Islands,[23] a man who also appears
in the life of Brigid of Kildare as a supportive mentor.

After some time Ibar left the Aran Islands to travel to Wexford in
the southeast of Ireland. Moninne and her companions traveled with
him. En route they spent time with Brigit in Kildare. For her companions
Moninne was "second only to Brigit in holiness of life, honesty of character and grace of virtues"[24] Many other fruitful encounters between like-
minded women are evoked by this briefly described episode in Moninne's
life. The strong and creative friendship that developed between Naomi
and Ruth across the difference of cultural origins is echoed as is the
encounter between Mary and Elizabeth from the Gospel of Luke, each
pregnant with her first child—one mother young, the other old, and both
full of joy and bafflement about the unfolding plan of God in their lives.
Moninne's encounter with Brigid evokes a sense of the need for creative
conversations with other visionary companions for those who wish to
move out the frontiers of spiritually grounded and committed lifestyles.

Moninne was empowered by her conversations with Brigit to give a
first expression to her personal calling and left Kildare to rejoin Ibar, who
in the meantime had become established in Beggary Island in Wexford.
This time, however, she joined him as a teacher. Ibar could provide the
support of the wise mentor in this first creative expression of her personal
vocation. Again, in this setting her profound capacity to connect with the
longings, hopes, and aspirations of the people of her time and country is
evident in the crowds that she draws: "not only women but also men de-
sired to join the holy nun; even if they were endowed with ample dignity,
they held it to be a great thing if they deserved to receive the blessing of
the very holy nun."[25] Parker Palmer in his notable book *The Courage to
Teach* has evocatively expanded the sense of vocation in teaching; "the

22. *The Life*, 69.

23. The motif of women religious innovators being educated by male mentors
is quite common in lives from this era. See Harrington, *Women in a Celtic Church*,
232–33.

24. *The Life*, 69.

25. *The Life*, 70.

things I teach are things I care about—and what I care about helps define my selfhood."[26]

Moninne's inspirational life did not, however, consist in a private holiness but also expressed itself in a deep compassion for those who were poor. The strength of this commitment was sometimes even a point of tension with some among her disciples, and there were complaints about the balance she exercised in the way she used communal resources since it sometimes seemed to excessively favor the poor visitor over her committed companions.[27] This reaction to the unfolding external expression of her inner spiritual insight reflects what is often a characteristic first stage in a creative development where comments like "It's an insane idea," or "it cannot be because it can never be!" may be prevalent. This stage is most difficult for a creative personality like Moninne, as it combines the difficulties of making a creative preference with the difficulties of finding misunderstanding and rejection in the social environment.

If the courage to live the vision can be found, a group solidarity and commitment among those attracted to the vision eventually emerges. This stage of development is illustrated by an event that occurred on Moninne's next journey, which ran from Wexford back to Kildare. Moninne and her traveling companions arrived at a river that suddenly became swollen as they approached to cross it, and so they were denied passage. The external block in their journey has a symbolic meaning in the story. It points to a lack of free-flowing communication in the group, and so Moninne inquired if anybody was hiding something from the group. One person in the group answered,[28] "As I was leaving the convent, I brought with me a handful of garlic."[29] Immediately when the declaration was made, the flood receded.

In the above symbolic incident we see that the companions of Moninnne were ultimately not companions of place or in possessions. Instead it is mutual trust, faith, and kindness that are the bonds of

---

26. Palmer, *The Courage to Teach*, 17.

27. *The Life*, 69–70.

28. According to Helen Noyes Webster, who interpreted the use of garlic on a journey in her book, *Herbs: How to Grow Them and How to Use Them*, the Israelites traveling with Moses missed the garlic they had in Egypt when they went toward the promised land because if Moses had carried garlic, the Israelites may have been able to avoid intestinal putrefaction from eating the desert's available lizards and snakes: "We remember the fish we used to eat in Egypt for nothing, the cucumbers, the melons, the leeks, the onions, and the garlic" (Numbers 11:5).

29. *The Life*, 71.

communion among the diverse women who spend time in her company in the various places where she lived. The priorities for Moninne are nurturing the bonds of inner spiritual communion over the outward rituals of a common life and sustaining the commitment to follow the call into an emerging future even in the face of obvious obstacles. What we witness in Moninne's life is more though than the predictable trajectory of a generic emerging movement. Her story reveals the process of birth for a group soul movement. Her return to Kildare for a second time at this point in the journey reveals the fundamental grounding of her itinerant vocation in soul dialogue with a wise mentor.

Having completed a spiritual internship with the leading teachers of her day, Moninne returns to her own territory in order to set down the foundations for her vision. The Christomorphic character of the enterprise on which she is embarking is symbolically represented in the biography through a narrative of changing water into wine. On two different occasions she is entertained by guests and in return creates a rich supply of wine or ale,[30] which endures even after her departure. In an analogous manner her life will be an abundant gift for others, since through solidarity with her people "excellent wine" is made abundantly available.

Moninne's life reflected insights which the modern British philosopher Bertrand Russell (1872–1970) articulated succinctly: "one of the symptoms of an approaching nervous breakdown is the belief that one's work is terribly important."[31] Thus, her relentless active solicitude for her own people, especially those who were poor or ill, is balanced in the biography with accounts of her immersion in desert space. The biographer refers to her as "the daughter of John the Baptist and the prophet Elias." This description is eremitically evocative as in Matthew's gospel (3:1–3) John's life is set "in the wilderness of Judea," while Elias (Elijah) from the tribe of Aaron was fed by ravens from God in the wadi Cherith (1 Kings 17).

Moninne's times of manifest solitude were spent "in prayer and vigils" and in general "follow[ed] in the footsteps of the earlier hermits."[32] Moninne exhibited the universal journey of insightful spiritual innovators by her withdrawal to solitary space. Entering the "desert" space symbolically represents the distance she placed between herself and the

---

30. Ibid., 72, 73.

31. Russell, *Conquest of Happiness*, 74.

32. *The Life*, 74.

established culture and life forms of her society. While there is much to learn from her daily engagements, it is in the silence that the learning is harvested, tasted, and digested. In the practice of removing herself from the busyness of her daily life she sought to embrace the wisdom that a creative indifference to the public symbols of success can yield.

The power of her prayer set her apart. Today there is a new appreciation of the power of the practices of prayer. Since Jon Kabat-Zinn established the mindfulness-based stress-reduction clinic at the Massachusetts Medical Center in 1979 and Herbert Benson established the Mind/Body Clinic of the Harvard Medical School at Boston Deaconess Hospital, the growth of research and publications in powerful spiritual practices for well-being such as pilgrimage, prayer, meditation, and solitude has been exponential. Moninne's life is an anticipatory archetype of the core gifts which spiritually committed lives offer to a society. Her life anticipates the contemporary concept of "spiritual capital."[33]

The reception of the religious innovation inaugurated through the movement she led is, however, conditioned by the consciousness of the times in which she lived. Her biographer therefore bestows the ultimate accolade on her spiritual genius by declaring that she had a man's soul in a woman's body.[34] The pervasive paradigm of the female person was that it was not holy but rather a frail and unreliable species. Gillian Cloke's extensive research on this subject concludes:

> anyone holy enough to be an exemplar of the faith could not *be* a woman: every one of the many who achieved fame through piety was held to "surpass her sex"—never, be it noted, to elevate the expectations that might be held of her sex. The argument is self-fulfilling: however many of this kind of women there were, in being superior they were always exceptional from their sex, never taken as representative; always regarded as a superior anomaly from their sex and in spite of it, and never as an example of their sex's capacity.[35]

Herein lies a salutary warning for women spiritual innovators. Religious systems continue to be predominantly male-managed. Women who seek to lead change movements in such systems can expect to

---

33. Verter, "Spiritual Capital," 150–74. O'Sullivan and Flanagan, *Spiritual Capital.*
34. Ibid.
35. Cloke, *This Female Man of God,* 220.

activate archetypal perceptions regarding the boundaries of woman's proper identity and role in the spiritual realm.

While the capacity to be spiritually innovative is a natural gift that Moninne enjoyed, it was also one she nurtured and developed through study and education. Maeve Callan's historical research has revealed that Moninne was known as "*doctissima abbatissa,* an exceptionally learned abbess."[36] She also recognized that the vitality of her spiritual movement depended on a well-educated membership. When she spots a natural gift of spiritual wisdom among those who participate in her movement she therefore encourages and supports their educational development. One incident in the life captures her commitment to the ongoing development of scholarship and learning in the group:

> Among the other handmaids of God, a nun by the name of Brignat is said to have lived with the holy nun (Darerca). Examining the signs of her future holiness, Darerca is said to have sent her to the island of Britain to learn the monastic rules at the monastery of Rostnat.[37] . . . Anxious to carry out the command of the holy mother, she stayed in a little inn by the aforementioned monastery where she perused the psalms and the other books which were necessary to her.[38]

The investment made in Brignat's development reveals Moninne's insight into the central place intellectual training has for the development of leadership for the future. The future of the spiritual vision that she had given expression to in her monastic foundation depended on the development of a honed imaginative capacity in her successors. Becoming familiar with expressions (rules) of spiritual initiatives similar to Killevy would enable future leaders to continuously renew so as to improve the service of the community in which they were embedded, detach from undesirable developments, and respond creatively to the unexpected.

One final incident that occurs close to the end of Moninne's life illustrates the central dynamic that was the root and sap of her flourishing foundation. Moninne shared her intuitive sense with her companions that there was a concealment of a compromising choice that a member of the group had made. She had no desire to use her leadership role to

---

36. Callan, "St. Darerca and Her Sister Scholars," 32.

37. For a discussion of whether the location of this monastery is in Galloway, Wales, or Cornwall, see Thomas, "Rosnat, Rostat, and the Early Irish Church," 100–106. [Ed.]

38. *The Life,* 75–76.

elicit the truth through fear-based injunctions. Instead, she enabled the group to realize that together they created sustaining intimacy within their common life. In the empathic atmosphere she created in the group, the withholding member came forward to acknowledge that she received a gift from a man with whom she had an affair.[39] Moninne's invitation to some in the group to assist their companion in the act of bringing her life into unity around her core commitment (through a ritual of supporting her in disposing of the gift) and Moninne's conclusion of the incident in a thanksgiving celebration all display profound insight into strategies for creating life-giving, sustainable spiritual community.

As was the case with Syncletica it is timely that Moninne's life has become available in a modern English translation for the first time when so many women are exploring forms of life that embrace solitude in new ways. From Moninne's life we see that her journey into creative solitude yielded:

- the establishment of a network of kindred women committed to socially alert soul work
- an appreciation of the benefit of learning for the spiritual journey
- a witness to the transforming power of a praying presence in a society

Interest in the spiritual legacy of Irish/Celtic countries has enjoyed huge popularity in recent times. While some of this interest focuses on what has been lost, there is also a parallel constructive movement. It is being recognized that the many Irish/Celtic holy men and women who set forth on unmapped journeys of spiritual innovation in their own society have much to teach those who find themselves on the threshold of the emergence of new forms of expressing the contemporary contemplative turn. Undertaking today's journey in the shadow of the company of these Celtic innovators provides inspiration, encouragement, and practical guidance.[40] Mary Margaret Funk, OSB, has creatively imagined what a future new expression of a Celtic-inspired monastic path might be by creating a dialogue between an Irish Abbess Bridget and a North American

---

39. Ibid., 76.

40. Ellis, *Celtic Women*; O'Loughlin, *Journeys on the Edges*; Meehan and Oliver, *Praying with Celtic Holy Women*.

Abbess Gertrude of a community focused on Christ Consciousness.[41]
The exchange is set in 2030 and it evocatively elicits a reexpression of
Moninne's contribution today.

41. Funk, "North Woods Abbey: On Lake Gogebic," in Hart, *A Monastic Vision for the 21st Century*, 199–224.

3

Mary of Oignies

Embracing Solitude in Medieval Flanders

THE EMINENT HISTORIAN OF Christian spirituality Bernard McGinn, in his comprehensive study of Christian mysticism, is "convinced from [his] previous reading and teaching that the year 1200 marked a major turning point,"[1] particularly with regard to new expressions of the intentional spiritual quest. One of the most numerous of these expressions for women was the beguine way of life.[2] The emergence of this way of life has long been viewed as "unusual" and "fascinating" because it cannot be traced to a single founding individual. Groups of like-minded women created a new spiritual life-form for themselves in response to changing culture circumstances. Indeed, today's observer of the Beguine movement might well describe the rapid simultaneous emergence in diverse locations of a similar type of religious trend as a good illustration of Malcolm Gladwell's "tipping point"[3] phenomenon. In his analysis of this phenomenon, Gladwell describes three stages in the emergence of even small changes in an environment that can precipitate a given change tipping over into widespread acceptance, endorsement, and/or enactment.

1. McGinn, *The Foundations of Mysticism* is first volume of a planned six-volume history of Christian mysticism. Volume 2, published in 1994, is titled *The Growth of Mysticism* (and treats the sixth through twelfth centuries). Volume 3, from 1998, is called *The Flowering of Mysticism: Men and Women in the New Mysticism* and spans 1200–1350. Volume 4, *The Harvest of Mysticism in Medieval Germany*, covers 1300–1500 and was released in 2005. Two volumes are forthcoming: *The Varieties of Vernacular Mysticism* and *The Crisis of Mysticism*.

2. There was a less numerous male equivalent known as the *beghard*. See McDonnell, *The Beguines and Beghards in Medieval Culture*.

3. Gladwell, *The Tipping Point*.

Some of the changes in the European medieval environment that scholarly theories have traditionally asserted contributed to the spectacular growth of the beguines were changing demographics, limitations for women on membership in monastic orders, and widespread religious fervor. The first of these theories, which asserts that the emergence of the Beguines reflects a rise in the number of single women in medieval European society due to the loss of men in wars and agricultural labor, is not widely accepted today. This lack of acceptance has arisen due to the inability to discover sufficient statistical data to make the case.[4] Carol Neel has extensively explored the second theory, which holds that restrictions placed on the membership of lay women religious in the Premonstratentians and Cistercians contributed to the growth of the Beguines. Neel sees the changing participation of lay women religious in traditional monastic orders as not occurring so dramatically as to give rise to an alternative religious lifestyle. "While early beguine life transgressed the boundary between laypersons and religious in an especially obvious fashion, that boundary had for a hundred years been eroded by the participation of lay brothers as well as lay sisters in reformed monasticism."[5]

Regarding the third influential factor in the emergence of the beguines (the flowering of a new mystical fervor), Bernard McGinn has shown how the foundational dynamics of this movement, which consisted in an enthusiasm for everyday mysticism, in a simplicity of life akin to the sort lived by the apostles during the earthly ministry of Jesus (*vita apostolica*), and in a new devotionalism were characteristic of beguine spirituality.

The most comprehensive historical account of the Beguines has been provided by Ernest McDonnell.[6] He has traced four eras in the history of the movement. Originally, in the later part of the twelfth century, diverse holy women with a common interest in religious experience— but without a formal communal structure—lived scattered throughout the cities of the Netherlands and Germany. The next phase commences

4. Murk-Jansen, *Brides in the Desert*, 22–23.

5. Neel, "The Origins of the Beguines," in Bennett et al., *Sisters and Workers in the Middle Ages*, 240–60; quotation on 256. At a wider level, the understanding of the emergence of the beguines, which required that the reason for their existence needed to be related to the phenomenon of traditional religious life, has limited the research into the origins of beguine life. See Mulder-Bakker "Introduction," in Eadem, *Mary of Oignies*, 3–30, especially 21ff.

6. McDonnell, *The Beguines and Beghards*.

toward the beginning of the thirteenth century. At this time the women began to organize into groups with leaders. There was a common commitment in the groups to service of the poor, to private devotion, to parochial worship and to chastity. In the third phase—which developed around the mid-thirteenth century—clusters of beguines began to gather around the ministries in which they served (hospices, schools, or infirmaries). Solitaries were also members of these clusters. In the final stage, which developed in the fourteenth century, the cluster of beguine dwellings became organized into self-contained village quarters (beguinages) with buildings for all the diverse dimensions of a collective spiritual life.

> The full-blown beguinage comprised a church, cemetery, hospital, public square, and streets and walks lined with convents for the younger sisters and pupils and individual houses for the older and well-to-do inhabitants. In the Great Beguinage at Ghent, with its walls and moats, there were at the beginning of the fourteenth century two churches, eighteen convents, over a hundred houses, a brewery, and an infirmary.[7]

Throughout the history of the Beguines certain core commitments were characteristic of the identity of the movement. In line with the *vita apostolica* ideal, frugality and simplicity of life were embraced. They provided for themselves not through endowment or inheritance but rather through the employment which they undertook. A spirituality of communion in mind and spirit was held in high esteem in the group. They gathered to discuss their spiritual experiences. These experiences had often been written down in their own vernacular. This journaling activity achieved an intimacy of revelation that discussions in a borrowed language (Latin) could not achieve in the same way. The prodigious analyst of medieval symbolism, Caroline Walker Bynum, has demonstrated how the charitable, the contemplative, and the ascetic aspects of Beguine life were unified in their writings through the theme of food.[8] Accounts of feeding miracles, eucharistic visions, and fasting, respectively, are pervasive in the accounts of the lives of Beguine women. The food practices of the women were often a locus of contestation where they protested the mindless consumption by the wealthy of their society, and where they announced solidarity with those who were hungry among their urban neighbors.

7. Ibid., 479.
8. Bynum, *Holy Feast and Holy Fast*, 115–29.

However, perhaps the most enduring aspect of the Beguine legacy is the distinctive character of the mysticism in which their lives were grounded, and it is this distinctive legacy that has prompted the inclusion of Mary of Oignies in the current selection. While the love mysticism characteristic of Beguine spirituality had been evident in Christian writers like Origen, Gregory of Nyssa, and Bernard of Clairvaux, it assumed a distinctive feminine form among the Beguines. The form of encounter with Christ that the phrase "love mysticism" encapsulates has a highly charged and deeply intense character in Beguine writings. The sexual imagery described in the recounted visions is often quite explicit, and there is no effort to allegorize the encounters, as happens in similar male mystical writings.[9] As Janet Ruffing has shown, love mysticism is not understood sympathetically even today, despite the great advances in the conceptual frameworks for appreciating the role of desire in moving religious expression.[10] It will not be surprising therefore that such passionate spirituality based on visions rather than biblical reflections provoked resistance—and sometimes scorn—for Beguine life

An appraisal from a contemporary religious observer, the Cistercian monk Caesarius of Heisterbach, sums up the beguine phenomenon positively, however. "Although these (holy) women, whom we know to be very numerous in the diocese of Liège, live among the people wearing lay clothes, they still surpass many of the cloister in the love of God. They live the eremitcal life among the crowds, spiritual among the worldly and virginal among those who seek pleasure."[11] In order to draw closer to the life and spirit of the women in this innovative solitude movement, we will now turn to the life of one of the early Beguines.

Mary of Oignies (1176–1213)

Bernard McGinn has asserted that "the archetype of the early stages of beguine life, and especially of beguine spirituality, is to be found in Mary of Oignies."[12] She was born in an economically comfortable family in Nivelles, which is forty kilometers south of Brussels. When she was fourteen, her life followed the pattern of her times, and her family arranged

9. Jantzen, *Power, Gender, and Christian Mysticism*, 133–40.

10. Ruffing, "Encountering Love Mysticism," 20–33.

11. Quoted in Simons, *Cities of Ladies*, 35.

12. McGinn, *The Flowering of Mysticism*, 33.

a marriage for her. Quite soon she and her husband, Jean, adopted some of the new spirituality trends of the surrounding culture, and they made a vow of chastity.[13] They turned all their energies to the service of the poor, destitute, and ill. A leprosarium on family lands at Willambroux became the particular focus for their service. In her early thirties Mary moved east to a house of Augustinian canons in Oignies (in the region of Namur). In her move to Oignies Mary separated amicably from her husband and acquired the support of a group of women who already lived a life similar in form to her own inspiration. In Oignies, further likeminded women began to be attracted by her expression of this new form of spiritual life which she had chosen. Over time the form of life that Mary created expanded to include more time for prayer. When she died at the age of thirty-six, she had not taken food for more than fifty days.

After Mary of Oignies died in June 1213, James of Vitry, who had come to know her as a soul friend, undertook to write her life.[14] He was a native of Champagne in the northeast of France and had heard of Mary's fame while he was a student in Paris. After a visit to her, he had joined the priory of regular canons in Oignies in order to be close to her. When James of Vitry (d. 1240), who in his own right was a famous preacher and later a cardinal, set about writing her life, he was entering into a long tradition of religious men creating the definitive historical record of exceptionally spiritually gifted women.[15] The biography by James has come to be recognized as a manifesto for the new form of intentional spiritual community that was being created by the beguines and that he firmly supported. Later James left Belgium to take up an episcopal position in the Holy Land. When travelling to take up this position, he visited the newly installed Pope Honorius III to request approval for the way of life undertaken by Mary and other holy women, a request that was partially successful.

13. James of Vitry dedicated the biography of Mary of Oignies to Bishop Fulk of Toulouse, who had visited Marie. He too had been married, but he and his wife had separated to follow their spiritual paths in religious communities. However, they had a family of two sons before making this decision; it was more common to have a family in a marriage before separating for spiritual purposes. See Elliott, *Spiritual Marriage*.

14. Dyan Elliottt has argued that the celebration of female spirituality in the thirteenth century by authors such as James of Vitry was part of a clerically sponsored church promotional activity: See chapter 2 (pp. 47–84) in Elliott, *Proving Woman*.

15. Coakley, *Women, Men, and Spiritual Power*. Chapter 4 discusses James's life of Marie, 68–88.

There were two main types of biographers of Beguine lives.[16] One group consisted of members of monastic orders, especially Cistercians. These writers often had limited contacted with Beguines other than the particular person for whom they were writing a biography. Some of these biographies were written by monastics to establish ecclesiastical control over the domain of work in which the Beguine was involved. James of Vitry's life of Mary, however, was of a different type and was informed by extensive conversations with diverse Beguines. Unlike the monastics, as a regular canon he had many opportunities to travel and meet diverse Beguines. These encounters yielded a sensitivity to the realities of the daily life Beguines lived and a sympathetic appreciation for the value of the form of life in its own right.

Mary's innovative way of ploughing the furrow of her life continues to attract contemporary women to lives embracing solitude. Themes in Mary's life overlap with insights from the lives of Syncletica and Moninne. First, each woman faced a challenging journey to incarnate her insights in a committed and spiritually focused way. Second, each woman tried to ground her spiritual initiatives in effective spiritual practices.

The most striking overlap in all three lives is the commentary on the reception of the women's initiatives by the systems in their cultures that sanctioned and ratified authentic spiritual movements. As in the lives of Moninne and Syncletica, so also in Mary's life there is an intense strength of emotion in Mary's disclosures about the way the male institutions of religion responded to her new initiatives. In paragraph 4 of the life of Mary, James de Vitry recalls "those shameless men who, hostile to all religion, maliciously slandered the ascetic life of these women (Beguines, including Mary) and, like mad dogs, railed against the customs which were contrary to theirs."[17] Two dynamics that beset movements of profound spiritual renewal are revealed here. First, those who follow the call they hear in their hearts, when this call is cast in an expression not previously known, can expect to face opposition, derision, misunderstanding, and ridicule. Second, James shares with readers the resources the women who were subjected to this experience used in order to make sense of it. They reminded themselves of parallel experiences in the lives of those in the Jesus movement as described in John's gospel: "if you belonged to the world, the world would love its own" (John 15:19).

16. Ibid., 37–38.

17. King and Feiss, *Two Lives of Marie d'Oignies*, 43.

As well as shedding light on her inward negotiation of external opposition, Mary's life also displays insightful recognition of the gendered
ground of the hostility and denigration experienced. James's account of
her life reflects Mary's inner turmoil generated by the double standards
used to evaluate the spiritual intent of men and women. In paragraph 22
James echoes, no doubt, a question Mary put to him as the pouring out
of her life in service was misunderstood: "Why are they [detractors] who
are not amazed at the worms which swarmed from the wounds of Simeon
and at the fire with which Antony burnt his feet not astonished at such
fortitude in the frail sex of a woman?"[18] Mary was obviously keenly aware
that the appreciative dispositions used to review the spiritual legacy of
the male desert religious innovators Simeon the Stylite and Antony of
Egypt would not be applied to her life of gospel service. Later in the life
(paragraph 41) James suggests that the problem encountered by Mary
and other Beguines of not achieving due recognition for the authenticity
of their spiritual innovation lay in the hegemony of left-brain, factual,
logical, ordered, hard knowledge over right-brain, intuitive, symbolic, affective, emotional wisdom. James challenges the "hard men" who "hear
and grumble" about the discourse of spiritual experience expounded by
Beguines to investigate their own affective knowledge of God and its con-
formity to the biblical vision of divine-human encounter, as set forth in
the Song of Solomon (4:11): "Your lips distil nectar, my bride."

Mary's life, like the other two that have been reviewed, has been
recorded because of the highly developed skills of spiritual discernment
she displayed. James is aware that capacities for spiritual awareness are
not highly valued and can easily be quenched. In paragraph 10 he sets out
his view of the value of recording her life.

> I have undertaken the present work . . . incited by its utility to
> many people. By so doing, I (hope that I) might, with the apos-
> tles, collect twigs with which I might heat myself and others,
> although I do not doubt that I too will be bitten by the serpent
> (cf. Acts 28:3) . . . There are many sensual people who do not
> have the Spirit of God . . . They deride and despise those things
> which they do not understand. The apostle spoke against them
> when he said, "Extinguish not the spirit, despise not prophecies"
> (1 Th 5:19, 20) . . . they scorn spiritual people, thinking them to
> be insane or idiots.[19]

18. King and Feiss, *Two Lives of Marie d'Oignies*, 63.

19. Ibid., 49.

Among the spiritual skills that Mary's life celebrates is the ability to be attentive to visions and dreams. In paragraph 35 we hear from James that "the Lord warned her in her dreams in the same way that he had warned Joseph and other saints and he visited his handmaid with many revelations." In attending to and honoring her visionary capacity Mary joins a long line of women mystics: Clare of Assisi, Catherine of Siena, Julian of Norwich and Joan of Arc, to name but a few. The essence of dream and visionary guidance and teaching is that it is rooted in metaphorical communication. According to distinguished linguists Lakoff and Johnson[20] metaphors, rather than merely being linguistic creations, are representations of the inner workings of the human person. The pervading presence of powerful dream symbols in Mary's life bespeaks the intense inner transformative journey through which she was passing and from which she so expertly guided others. The form of communal, spiritual life of which she is a foundational member is not simply an external expression of spiritual aspirations but an external creation in the public forum of the world she already occupied intensely.

The highly transformative inner process through which Mary passed during the course of her life is made present in the text of her life through the frequent accounts of her weeping and tears:

> Both day and night her eyes continuously brought forth outpourings of the waters which fell not only on her cheeks but also on the church floor, and lest her tears make the ground all muddy, she caught them in the veil with which she covered her head. She used up so many veils in this manner that she often had to change her wet veil for a dry one. (paragraph 18)[21]

The presence of episodes of transformative weeping in lives of sincere spiritual seekers from the Christian tradition can be traced across the millennia.[22] One of the most notable examples is John Climacus (c. 579–649). John was a member of a desert community at the foot of Mount Sinai, where most of his life was spent as a solitary. In the instructive text he wrote after being appointed leader of the cenobitic group in his community, *The Ladder of Ascent*, there is extensive commentary on

---

20. Lakoff and Johnson, *Metaphors We Live By*.

21. King and Feiss, *Two Lives of Marie d'Oignies*, 60.

22. Patton *Holy Tears*. Alan Jones also has an excellent chapter devoted to this topic in *Soul Making*, 82–106, as has Christie, *The Blue Sapphire of the Mind*, 70–101.

the phenomenon of tears.[23] *The Ladder of Ascent* is the most copied book in Eastern Christian spirituality, apart from the Bible, and so its teaching has been tested by generations of pilgrims on the spiritual journey. John Climacus prefaces his teaching on tears[24] by advising the spiritual guide that tears are hard to analyze because they can come about in a variety of ways. What appears critical in understanding the tears of a directee is to have a knowledge of the interior disposition of the person who is weeping. Tears arising in ordinary and natural settings of pain or loss can be a moment of awakening to the deeper spiritual significance of events. Likewise John Climacus advises that if one is not on a spiritual journey then it is necessary to beware of tears," for wine drawn straight from the presses cannot be trusted."[25] His insights regarding the interpretation of tears have roots going back into the psalms. There we see that profound inability to see God at work in one's life can provoke tears:

> I eat ashes like bread,
>
> and mingle tears with my drink
>
> because of your indignation and anger
>
> for you have lifted me up and thrown me aside (Ps 102:9–10)

Elsewhere, the struggle to live by faith in tragically changed life circumstances can be the trigger for tears:

> Be gracious to me O God for I am languishing;
>
> O Lord, heal me, for my bones are shaking with terror . . .
>
> I am weary with moaning;
>
> Every night I flood my bed with tears;
>
> I drench my couch with my weeping. (Ps 6:2, 6)

Today there is a new understanding of how the entire person is a vehicle (especially the embodied dimension of personhood are vehicles) of spiritual encounter and awakening.[26] In this context Mary of Oignie's tears challenge another dimension of the lives of those pursuing the God quest on behalf of society. No aspect of human life is outside that quest,

---

23. Luibheid and Russell, trans. *The Ladder of Divine Ascent*. Cynthia Bourgeault has identified some of the limitations arising from the image of the ladder for teaching contemplative practice. See Bourgeault, *Centering Prayer and Inner Awakening*, 70–71.

24. Luibheid and Russell, *The Ladder of Divine Ascent*, 139–40.

25. Ibid., 140.

26. Patton, *Holy Tears*; Anderson, "Nine Psycho-Spiritual Characteristics of Spontaneous and Involuntary Weeping," 167–73.

and an openness to embodied expression of spiritual longing has a proper place in the spiritual journey. It behoves those in life forms focused on learning the science of nurturing life in the Spirit to become personally familiar with spontaneous and involuntary embodied responses to the sense of the Holy, such as weeping.

Mary's wisdom and understanding in the face of psychosomatic-spiritual phenomena was one of the exceptional personal characteristics that set her apart. One incident in paragraph 31 of her life captures this gift with dramatic effect. A young woman in a local Cistercian monastery was deeply troubled by the thoughts and images arising from her maturing sexual identity, and the clash they posed for her with her religious commitments.

> Unaccustomed to such things, she was terrified and at the very moment that the thought occurred to her, she imagined that she had lost her faith, even though she resisted it with great sorrow for a long time and sorrowed greatly. She, however, was not able to endure it since she did not open the wound of her heart to anyone to receive a medicine and she therefore fell into despair because of her faint-heartedness.[27]

Modern studies of the healing of inner wounds[28] illuminate the power of Mary's intervention in this story, whereby the woman was restored to fullness of well-being after her conversations with Mary. The inability to speak of her wound to another person may reveal a prior history of soul wounding in which the young woman had learned to hide her feelings of powerlessness, doubt, dismay, or inadequacy. Her capacity for care seeking had been damaged. Mary, however, could reach into that wounded place and "received her kindly both in her cell and in her heart." Such unequivocal understanding and care communicated deeply to the troubled woman that she was not alone. Instead, it embodied Mary's spiritual healing power wherein she placed a hand of kindness on these inner wounds. Her healing actions were testimony to the wisdom she had gained from her wrestling with her own demons.

Another recurrent theme in Mary's life bespeaks the deep inner peace from which she approached life. Paragraph 41 is illustrative, where we are told that "the expression of her face enabled many people . . . to

---

27. King and Feiss, *Two Lives of Marie d'Oignies*, 72.

28. Grant, *The Way of the Wound*.

obtain the grace of devotion by looking at her."[29] This image from Mary's life acts as a reminder of the scene of the Transfiguration where the Gospel recounts how when Jesus was praying, the appearance of his face changed (Luke 9:29). It can in turn be compared to the scene where Moses returned from the mountain, having had an encounter with God, and Aaron with all the Israelites saw Moses's face was radiant (Exod 34:30). In more recent times Thérèse of Lisieux expressed the quality of inspiration from the face of Jesus in the prayers and poems she wrote for various occasions. Her shortest prayer[30] requested, "Make me resemble you, Jesus!" She wrote these words on a small card to which she attached a stamp of the face of Jesus. The natural occurrence on the spiritual journey of mirroring (the development of an image resemblance between God and the human person) is scattered through many texts of the Christian spiritual traditions.[31] The spiritual journey leads into the knowledge of the love, kindness, and compassion of God. Love produces likeness; as persons experience themselves being empathetically held by God, so persons hold their own selves more empathically and live in the world with a kindness reflected in their physiognomy.

Compassion was evident not only in Mary's appearance. She also displayed loving-kindness in her actions. Paragraph 55 of her life paints her practical love in a series of seven scenes of successful healing interventions on behalf of critically ill people. The concluding paragraph explains that these healings were not accomplished purely on the basis of a clinical evaluation and response. Rather, prayer was central to Mary's work of healing. Contemporary empirical experiments that investigate the impact of prayer on healing suggest that the love of the one making the prayer for an ill person is an important factor in the successful outcome of the prayer.[32] Mary's life anticipates the new conversation between health and spirituality, which is accumulating ever increasing significance today.[33]

In the life of Mary a final noticeable feature is the cultural formation of the spirituality by which she lived. Each historical era and context in the history of spirituality has unique expressions of spirituality that come

29. King and Feiss, *Two Lives of Marie d'Oignies*, 84.

30. Gaucher, *The Prayers of Saint Thérèse of Lisieux*, 11.

31. Seelaus, "Traditions of Spiritual Guidance: The Self-Mirror of God."s

32. Dossey, *Prayer Is Good Medicine*, 105.

33. Bouwer, *Spirituality and Meaning in Health Care*.

to the fore. For Mary's era the uniqueness was often expressed through food practices. In paragraph 87 we see that at times, "she hungered for God with a wondrously changing affectivity and at other times she thirsted for him."[34] However, the management of the embodied dimension of this experience posed difficulties for her, and James reminds us that "she was constricted and all dried up from her long fasts and sometimes it was difficult for her to eat. She suffered pain from a cold and constricted stomach and she would become bloated by only a little food which she would then spit out."[35] But this account is not unique to her life, and as noted already Caroline Walker Bynum has provided an extensive account of how "extreme fasting is a theme in every female *vita* from the Low Countries."[36]

Bynum asserts that the modalities of spirituality and practices of women medieval mystics are not what need to be replicated today, but instead "they can point the direction in which we should search."[37] One contemporary issue that food attachment in medieval spirituality points to is a tendency in much contemporary popular spiritual literature and seminars to focus on achieving detachment, sometimes artificially.[38] The widespread contemporary turn to Buddhist practices of nonattachment may lead the spiritual seeker to fall prey to the danger of becoming attached to nonattachment, when these seekers do not have access to the traditions and guidance that Buddhist teachers provide. Just as Mary's practices ultimately robbed the world of her contribution when she was thirty-six, so today seekers overattached to nonattachment could end up practicing a socially disengaged spirituality, deaf to the cry of those who suffer.

It is a well developed practice in leadership training programs today to learn about leadership from the lives of innovators and entrepreneurs. Lives like that of Mary d'Oignies therefore provide unique assistance in negotiating new spiritual developments. She had no map to follow. She attended carefully to her inner drawings, and trusted what she was intuiting through her dreams. She forged he journey in conversational

34. King and Feiss, *Two Lives of Marie d'Oignies*, 130.

35. Ibid., 64.

36. Bynum, *Holy Fast and Holy Feast*, 119.

37. Ibid., 302.

38. Tolle, *The Power of Now*; Bstan-Dzin-Rgya-Mtsho (Dalai Lama XIV) and Lopez, *The Way to Freedom*; Sogyal, *The Tibetan Book of Living and Dying*; Trungpa, *The Myth of Freedom and the Way of Meditation*.

relationship with diverse people. She adapted and changed as new circumstances presented themselves. In all of this Mary provides encouragement and guidance for the new expressions of committed religious life emerging at this time.

Beguines and the Future

There has been a flowering of interest in the spiritual legacy of the Beguines in recent times.[39] Their story ignites the imagination. In becoming familiar with their innovative spiritual enterprise we are invited to imagine what shape such a bold, new adventure might take today. Their lives are a challenge because they display the same type of daring courage seen in the midwives who preserved Moses from death (Exod 1:15–21), despite the opposition and danger they faced from the Pharaoh. Similarly, the Beguines did not find the right course of action in their lives by requesting the authorities of their society to ratify their actions. Instead, the Beguines risked following what was in their hearts and left space for God to nurture the seed sown in good faith.

---

39. Grundmann, *Religious Movements in the Middle Ages*; McGinn, *Meister Eckhart and the Beguine Mystics* (chapter 6); Malone, *Women and Christianity*, Vol. 2, *The Medieval Period AD 1000–1500* (chapter 5).

4

Angela Merici
Embracing Solitude in Renaissance Italy

JUST AS SIGNIFICANT SOCIAL changes in the European medieval environment contributed to the spectacular growth of the Beguines, so the rise of a new religious enthusiasm among Italian women, expressed in the Company of Saint Ursula, which Angela Merici founded, can be traced to socio-historical events. Various disasters had befallen Italy, including an invasion by the French king Charles VIII in November 1494. In this and other invasions, crops were destroyed, great brutality was visited upon local populations, and women were often the victims of rape. Religious revival was a communal exercise in resilience in this context of oppression. The religious spirit of sixteenth-century Italy was also shaped by the various alternative Christian groups that had grown in strength and numbers during the previous centuries. In the north of Italy where Angela lived the Waldensians had a strong presence. The Waldensians were a popular group who encouraged personal holiness without ecclesiastical rituals. Alberto Margoni, in his analysis of Angela Merici's spirituality, proposes that there was a readiness for her spiritual giftedness in an environment where new movements had sown the seeds of spiritual seeking.[1]

Angela's imaginative construction of a new spiritually focused life-form for women has similarities to the emergence of the beguines in the Low Countries, presented in the previous chapter. There were also Italian precedents from which she could draw inspiration, such as the *bizzoche*

---

1. Margoni, *Angela Merici*, 8.

movement,[2] which consisted of single male recluses or pairs of female recluses withdrawing from society in pursuit of the spiritual journey, or the *pinzoccheri,* which referred to those who followed a regimen of spiritual practices in their own homes, including being committed to evangelical poverty and celibacy, but without taking formal vows. Other women, known as *cellane,* sought seclusion in their own homes or in small dwellings attached to churches. What Angela eventually created, however, was different from all these. Below we will see how her intentional attention to the wisdom of the heart culminated in a way of spiritual living with a distinctive nuptial spirituality at its core, rather than the spirituality of acts of service that informed many other contemporary analogous developments.

Angela's Life (1474–1540)

Angela Merici was born in a setting of great natural beauty in the north of Italy, where the Alpine slopes were part of the landscape that formed her identity, as well as the expansive water scenery of the Lake Garda. The town where she was born, Desenzano, lies to the south west of Lake Garda. Her birth is usually dated to the first five years of the 1470s. She grew up with three brothers and a sister.[3] A friend from her later life recorded some of her memories of these early years,[4] particularly her recollections from the lives of saints read to her as a child. The family's social situation was relatively comfortable, as they garnered their living from trading in their hometown, which was a busy center of Italian commerce.

During Angela's teenage years her father, mother, and sister died in quick succession of each other. These events ruptured the horizons of consciousness within which she had lived up to that time. During the years following these bereavements Angela was catapulted into a renegotiation

---

2. The *Bizzoche* Movement was widespread in thirteenth-century Italy. M. Sensi, "Anchoresses and Penitents in Thirteenth- and Fourteenth-Century Umbria," in Bornstein and Rusconi, *Women and Religion in Medieval and Renaissance Italy,* 56–83, especially 64–67.

3. The debate regarding Angela's family history and composition is ongoing. See Mariani et al., *Angela Merici,* 88–99.

4. This information comes from an account of Angela's life known as *Processo Nazari.* This account was written in 1568 by the notary Giovan Battista Nazari de Sayani. It was a compilation of eyewitness information which he had taken under oath from four close associates of Angela.

of the purpose of her life and a search for the meaning of these deaths, especially that of her sister, who was her friend and companion. As Julian of Norwich's traumatic grief during the Black Death formed the context within which her unique spiritual visionary insights and commitments came to pass, so it was with Angela. During her time of grief Angela was living with the family of her mother's brother.

One day while she was alone in the fields, it seemed to her that the skies opened and she experience the company of angels and young girls of her sister's age, including one whom she identified as her sister. There was a moment of stillness in the vision when her sister stepped forward to her and spoke to her of her calling to gather young women together in dedication to God. As had been the case with countless prophets and saints who had gone before her, Angela came to know in embracing this experience her unique spiritual calling from God, and throughout her entire life she sought to be true to this annunciation.[5] It was immensely challenging to experience the burden of being called to put women at the center of her endeavors. The lives of women in Italy at that time were bespoken; they were exchanged in marriage arrangements or given to convents. How could she possibly interfere with the social order? Her early biographers believed that she needed the promptings of further mystical experiences and deep pondering on the innovative wisdom guiding her before she gave expression to her unique, personal call towards the end of her time on earth in her *Rule of Life*.[6]

Angela did not make an immediate, distinctive, and radical response to what she had learned about her personal vocation. Instead, she followed a path that was chosen by many of her contemporaries and became a member of the third order of Franciscans in Salò, the town where she had gone to live with her uncle after the deaths in her family. This choice had beneficial outcomes socially. It left her free from pressure to marry. This choice also provided her with personal space to deepen her spiritual journey within the supportive environment of like-minded companions.

Later Angela returned to the town where she had grown up with her family. The return to her hometown marked another letting go of familiar external supports and so pushed her to turn inwards again in order to clarify the contours of the journey gradually emerging into her consciousness. In this attentive attunement she experienced guidance

5. The historical document on which this account is Teresa Ledochowska OSU, *Angela Merici and the Company of Saint Ursula*, 1:16.

6. Mariani et al., *Angela Merici*, 254–55.

through a visual insight for a second time. In this significant moment of guidance for her journey Angela's insight assumed the form of the ancient biblical symbol of the ladder, which was present in Jacob's dream at Bethel (Gen 28:10–15). The highly evocative nature of the symbol of the ladder is reflected in the title of a famous seventh-century spiritual classic, *The Ladder of Divine Ascent,* written by John Climacus.[7] In this classic the symbol of the *ladder* represents a core teaching regarding the spiritual journey; the ladders is a reminder that the journey is not something completed all at once through a jump or leap but requires instead a willingness to allow one step to gradually lead to the next movement in an emerging consciousness. In her visual insight Angela was aware of young women moving up along the ladder. Intuitively she sensed that her call would lead her to provide leadership for women seeking to lead lives with spiritual intention.[8]

When Angela was approximately forty years of age she moved again—this time to Brescia. This move happened in response to a request put to her by the Franciscans in Salò. Caterina Patengola, who was part of the spiritual community of the Franciscans in Salò, had lost her husband and three children in quick succession and was overwhelmed with grief. Caterina was almost the same age as Angela and lived in Brescia, fifteen miles west of Lake Garda. Angela's support to Caterina would have the benefit of being grounded in Angela's own experiences of traumatic multiple losses, and in a common attentiveness to the transcendent questions posed by loss.

While staying with Caterina, Angela met Giovan Antonio Romano, one of the many young business friends of Caterina's sons who visited the Patengola household. When Caterina was making progress in recovering from her grief, Antonio provided Angela with personal quarters, which gave Angela some solitude to consider the direction of her life amid the many invitations she was receiving to provide spiritual guidance. Antonio had extensive conversations about the meaning of life with her and introduced several of his friends to her, within a context where they were trying to come to terms with the terrible slaughter and destruction that had befallen Brescia in the immediately preceding years at the hands of French mercenaries. Many of these friends belonged to a religious

---

7. Luibheid and Russell, trans., *The Ladder of Divine Ascent.*

8. An intuitive reading of Angela Merici's legacy has been created by M. C. Durkin, *Angela Merici's Journey of the Heart.*

philanthropic movement called *Compagnia del Divino Amore.*[9] As well as conversational relationships becoming a cornerstone of her spiritual quest, so also pilgrimage became a significant means for Angela to search for what she was truly called to do with the remaining years of her life.

In 1520 when she was forty-six years old, she traveled a short distance southwards to Mantua to pray at the tomb of the Blessed Osanna Andreasi, a wealthy woman Dominican tertiary who shared the same type of spiritual acuity that characterized Angela's life. In undertaking this journey Angela reflected an intuitive appreciation of the communion of saints which the contemporary feminist theologian Elizabeth Johnson has described as the "companionship of friends." Johnson views this friendship paradigm as an egalitarian approach to the remembered cloud of witnesses who serve the community as inspiration and encouragement on its own journey of faith.[10] Angela's pilgrimage seems to bespeak her own confidence in the possibility of obtaining support and guidance, even across the chasm of death, from those who had gone ahead of her on a similar journey in uncertainty as her own.

Angela made another important pilgrimage when she was fifty years of age. She set sail for the Holy Land with some other pilgrims. She was accompanied by her cousin and by Antonio Romano. The port of departure for the Holy Land was Venice. Her days in Venice before departure provided her and her companions an opportunity to connect with Venetian lay brotherhoods, many of whom sponsored the religious paintings of the city's artists. It may have been through these meeting that her connection with St. Ursula was reignited since the fifteenth-century Venetian artist Vittore Carpaccio had created a series of nine paintings depicting the legend of St. Ursula[11] through the sponsorship of a lay brotherhood in Venice.

---

9. The *Compagnia del Divino Amore* was founded by Ettore Vernazza in Genoa in 1497. The members of the confraternity combined spiritual development with philanthropy. See Black, *Italian Confraternities in the Sixteenth Century*, 29.

10. Johnson, *Friends of God and Prophets*, 175.

11. The Feast of Saint Ursula and Her Companions was removed from the Roman Catholic calendar of saints in 1969. Multiple diverse versions of accounts of her fifth-century life exist. Typically, Ursula is described as the beautiful daughter of a Christian British king who was promised in marriage to a pagan prince against her wishes. In a dream she was advised to demand as a condition of marriage a delay of three years, during which time she and her numerous female companions would have the opportunity to travel. They visited Rome and then traveled to Cologne in Germany where they were martyred during a battle with the Huns that was taking place.

During the sea crossing the pilgrimage assumed a new form. In Crete, on the way to the Holy Land, Angela lost her sight almost completely. Many of the sights which she visited in the Holy Land therefore made an interior rather than exterior impact. The inner intensity of emotion that the pilgrimage evoked overflowed at the scene of the Crucifixion where she shed many tears. Towards the end of the journey Angela's sight was completely restored. The experience of illness that beset Angela during the Holy Land pilgrimage is evocative of the contemporary concept of "creative illness."[12] Such illnesses are usually sudden and clearly defined. The person who passes through a creative illness is energized with a creative impulse that will go on to express itself in innovative contributions to the worlds in which they are located and that spread out beyond that world also.

The energy that Angela gained from the Holy Land pilgrimage, despite the huge physical demands that such traveling made in the sixteenth century, is evident in Angela's decision to go to Rome the following year. This trip afforded her an opportunity to visit the basilicas and catacombs and to be inspired by the witness of the lives remembered at the various sites. The records of her life indicate that she had an audience with the Pope during this trip. At this audience she was invited to establish her loving outreach to the people of the city of Rome, but her heart drew her back to Brescia. Angela's spirit of seeking out the direction she was called to take in her life continued to express itself in her frequent pilgrimages, in the expansion of her diverse circle of associates, and in her service to the poor of the Brescia.

When she returned to Brescia, she changed accommodations on a number of occasions, finally settling in a house near the Church of Saint Afra. Her energy for travel and for extending the circles of conversation in her life was intense during these years. Eventually this led in 1531 to inviting a group of twelve women friends, from diverse social backgrounds to co-establish with her a new expression of intentional commitment to the spiritual journey. One of the first undertakings of this new group of Angela and her twelve companions was to make a pilgrimage to the Holy Mount of Varallo, in the foothills of the Alps, almost one hundred miles north of Brescia. This was a Franciscan shrine where a series of small chapels had been built to remember the holy sites in Bethlehem and Jerusalem.

---

12. Ellenberger, "The Concept of Creative Illness," 442–56.

More women joined the companions over the next four years and the initiative of vowed commitment to the values of religious life in a context of living at dispersed locations in Brescia was gradually clarified. On the feast of Saint Catherine of Alexandria, 25th November 1535, the Company of Saint Ursula was formally established in collaboration with twenty-eight women associates at a ceremony in the Church of St. Afra,. To clarify the ideals and purpose of this new expression of spiritual community, Angela, who was now sixty-one years of age, designed a *Rule of Life* (Regola) through a process of dialogue and discussion and with the assistance of Gabriele Cozzano, who provided legal and business support to the fledgling group. The Rule was approved in 1536 by the ecclesiastical authorities of Brescia. In March 1537, Angela was elected the leader of the group for life.

It would not be appropriate, however, to convey the impression that a seamless trajectory progressing from strength to strength was characteristic of Angela's experience. There were instead multiple challenges. Many of those from whom she might have expected understanding or support were not shy in expressing their resistances in the form of reservations, or in leveraging their social power to ferment opposition. Negative comments from leaders in Brescian society sowed seeds of doubt in the minds and hearts of some members, and so there were departures from the group. Others who were disturbed by the negative commentary moved to the more recognizable form of religious life that monastic communities provided. Among those who stayed there were sometimes efforts to move the project closer to an expression of classical religious life recognizable within Italian society of that time.

In 1539, when the membership of the group was reaching 150, Angela sensed that her life was coming to an end, and she worked with her secretary, Gabriel Cozzano, to write two further documents. One of the documents is commonly referred to as *Counsels* (*Ricordi*). It set forth in nine Counsels her vision for how leadership would function within the context of dispersed living. Much of the wisdom that she shares with the Colonelli (leaders of geographical districts) bears a remarkable resemblance to innovative contemporary leadership theory. One typical example may be found in the eighth counsel. Angela advises the leaders, "Love all your daughters equally and do not show preference for one more than another, because they are all God's children and you have no idea of what He wishes to make of them."[13] Similarly, the contemporary

13. *Counsels and Legacies* were dictated by Angela Merici to her scribe,

leadership trainer Margaret Wheatley calls leaders to live with the truth that "once the system emerges, it can't be changed by analysing its individual members or by singling them out for removal. We can't change a system by changing individuals."[14] The second document that comes from the final months of Angela's life is the *Testament* (*Testamento* or *Legati*). It is directed to the nine Lady Governors (the matrons/trustees) and creates an innovative mechanism whereby a trust body oversees the temporal well-being of the group in a spirit attuned to the core spiritual values of the group that Angela established. Of the three documents left by Angela, it is the *Rule* that provides most insight into her vision of daily gospel living within the framework of a spirituality of communion nurtured among those who live in their own homes.

Two practices for entering the cave of the heart stand out from all others in the life of Angela of Merici—the practices of soulful conversation and pilgrimage. In a previous publication[15] I have noted that Thomas Clancy, in his monograph *The Conversational Word of God*,[16] has performed an invaluable service in retrieving the perennial significance of the practice of conversation in the ministry and spirituality of the Christian community. In particular, he has shown the central place of conversation in the spirituality and ministry of Ignatius of Loyola, as well as in those of his companions Francis Xavier and Pierre Favre. When Diego Laynez, one of Ignatius's first companions, remembered the early days of the Society of Jesus in Paris, he remarked that frequent visits to their various gathering places for the purpose of conversation helped them all a great deal. But as well as the practice of conversation building the bonds of companionship, it also served as an effective practice in ministry. Indeed one of the distinctive emphases of the Ignatian legacy is the prominence it gives to conversation.

Two aspects of Ignatius's instruction regarding conversation may be helpful to consider if conversational practice, so evident also in the life and ministry of Angela Merici, is to be retrieved as a means of companioning the spiritual awakening happening in Western society today. First, Ignatius was clear that conversation must begin around the issues at the fore for people: we have to go in by our neighbor's door. Second, Ignatius

---

Gabriele Cozzano, around 1539–40. Angela's Eight Counsels is here taken from Stone, *Commentary*.

14. Wheatley and Myron Kellner-Rogers, *A Simpler Way*, 78.

15. Flanagan, "Sitting Spirituality," 20–29.

16. Clancy, "*The Conversational Word of God.*"

encouraged those engaged in the ministry of conversation to take the time needed to really understand how things appeared from the other person's point of view. The other person's hopes, anxieties, and desires are the motions of new life growing but are susceptible to being easily crushed in their fragility. While the contribution of Ignatius of Loyola to establishing the place of conversation in coming to know the way of the Spirit is well known today, the living practice of Angela Merici is a kindred response in the society in which she was immersed.

The second practice for entering the cave of the heart—pilgrimage—is illumined by recent developments in pilgrimage anthropology[17] as a science. This enables the contemporary reader of Angela Merici's story to appreciate more deeply how undertaking pilgrimage enabled Angela to separate from whatever rigidities might have developed in her daily life and empowered her repeatedly to step into a world of unexplored horizons. After each of her pilgrimages she returned with a new vitality and clarity of vision to the urban centers where she lived. "The pilgrimage ritual, regardless of religious tradition, ultimately "dramatizes the quest for the divine" by means of holistic engagement with an ancient process of transformation."[18] In an article entitled "From Pilgrimage to Crusade" Thomas Merton reflected on the idea of geographical pilgrimage as "the symbolic acting out of an inner journey," then set this in contrast to inner journey that was "the interpolation of the meanings and signs of the outer pilgrimage," and concluded by noting that though it would be possible to have a geographical pilgrimage without an inner journey and vice versa, it is "best to have both."[19] In the records of the outward journeys made by Angela across her life span, we see a woman who is restless in her pursuit of that Spirit calling her to take another step on the ladder to God, so evocatively captured in the originating vision of her call to embrace solitude of heart.

17. Morinis, *Sacred Journeys*; Turner and Turner, *Image and Pilgrimage in Christian Culture*; Coleman, *Reframing Pilgrimage*.

18. Kelly, "Pilgrimage and Spiritual Capital," in O'Sullivan and Flanagan, *Spiritual Capital*.

19. Merton, "From Pilgrimage to Crusade," in *Mystics and Zen Masters*, 91–112, at 92.

The Rule of Life of Angela Merici

The importance of Angela Merici's legacy for discussions of a form of women's new monasticism is unique and unrivaled. In the other lives discussed, it was necessary to exercise a hermeneutic of reconstruction with regard to vision of the women for the lives they were living since their biographies had been written by men. In Angela's case insights gleaned from her life story can be complemented and enriched by putting them in dialogue with the *Rule of Life* that she herself created. As noted, Angela wrote her *Rule* in collaboration with a male associate and scribe, Gabriele Cozzano. The rule received diocesan approval in 1536 and papal approval in 1546. Various subsequent revisions, as well as the imposition of a classical monastic way of life on later companions of Angela Merici, resulted in the loss of access to the original rule until the 1920s when an edition of the rule dating back to 1545 was found in the Trivulzian Library in Milan.

The Rule underwent the kind of changes that reflect the ancient pervasive requirement that women's lives reflect adequate submission to ecclesiastical authorities. Some of the changes introduced put greater emphasis on living in groups and engaging in works such as the teaching of religion. The issuing of Pius V's *Circa pastoralis* (1566) and *Lubricum vitae genitus* (1568), which resulted in the outcome that women who wished to be recognized as religious had no other option but to become enclosed, inevitably influenced the lived form of Angela's original inspiration.[20] The version of the rule that will be used in the discussion below will be based on the oldest version available and will not reflect later changes.

This presentation of Angela's rule also takes account of the scarcity of resources available to her for writing such a rule. Documents that provide guidance for women's common spiritual journey were rare, and those written by women were even rarer. In the twelfth-century France the philosopher monk Abelard had received a request from his once wife and then co-pilgrim in religious life, Heloise (1101–1162), to compose a rule of life specifically for women.[21] He reluctantly composed a text, but it did not become part of the life of Heloise's Benedictine community. Other twelfth-century efforts to feminize the living practice of religious life included the writing of the *Speculum virginum* (*A Mirror for Virgins*)

---

20. Lux-Sterritt, *Redefining Female Religious Life.*

21. Georgianna, "'In Any Corner of Heaven,'" in Wheeler, *Listening to Heloise,* 187–216.

and the *Hortus deliciarum* (*The Garden of Delights*). The *Speculum* has the style of a dialogue between a monk, Peregrinus, and a nun, Theodora. It was created by a monk from South Germany around 1140, and its purpose was to create greater understanding among men who provided spiritual guidance or instruction to vowed women of the particular character of the female spiritual journey.[22] The *Hortus* is a visual exposition of the theological, philosophical, and cultural issues of the day to a German Augustinian community of women by a woman, the community's prioress Herrad.[23]

A century later the Italian woman Clare of Assisi (1193–1253) tirelessly confronted the challenges of articulating a way of religious life as a woman for women. In this task she confronted a succession of setbacks from popes (Honorius III, Gregory IX, and Innocent IV) determined to regularize women's religious life in order to supervise the diversity of free-spirited groups springing up. Throughout her life Clare and her companions stayed true to the inspiration that they had received, and in her final hours of life in August 1253, she finally received pontifical approval for the rule she had written. The rule, *The Form of Life of Clare of Assisi*, was the first written by a woman to receive papal approval.[24] Birgitta of Sweden (1303–1373) also made a significant contribution to creating a woman's rule of life, though her rule was not gleaned from lived experience in the same was as Clare's, but emerged instead from religious insight that she affirmed as a utterly unexpected gift. A modified version of Birgitta's monastic Rule (*Regula salvatoris*) received its first formal approbation in 1370, and the Birgittine Order was formally recognized posthumously in 1378 by Pope Urban VI.[25]

The difficulties for Clare, Birgitta, and other women attempting to write rules of life were compounded by a decree issued by the Fourth Lateran Council in 1215—*Ne nimia religionum*—which legislated that any new religious communities had to follow one of the approved rules: Benedict, Augustine, or Francis. The process of institutionalizing the charismatic endeavors of women (and some men) in pursuit

22. Mews, *Listen Daughter*.

23. The three efforts to feminize the practice of religious life described in this paragraph arose in the context of a wider unease in the medieval period about the proper provision for the care of religious women (*Cura mulierum*) See McNamara, *Sisters in Arms*, chapter 10.

24. McNamara, *Sisters in Arms,* 307–10.

25. Morris, *St. Birgitta of Sweden*, 145–48.

of permanently-committed gospel living continued intensely until the Council of Trent, which issued *Decretum de regularibus et monalium* in 1563.[26] Over the course of these developments the legal status of religious women became the core defining factor of the identity of women seeking to be spiritual companions in a formal group arrangement. The era of "pernicious," "quasi-religious," women had come to an end.[27]

When the existence of Angela's rule is considered against such a hostile environment, it is an astonishing achievement. What is immediately evident when one first reads the *Rule* of Angela Merici[28] is its obvious emotional warmth. Earlier I commented on how the Counsels for the leaders among the companions displayed an appreciation of emotional intelligence equivalent to what one commonly finds in contemporary leadership training programs. Similarly, right from its opening announcement the *Rule* is steeped in affective depth and strength. Angela addressed it to "figliole et sorelle dilettissime" ("daughters and beloved sisters") and so by her affectionate adjectival inclusion sets the stage for atmosphere of empathic interaction among the companions.[29] Intuitively Angela seems to understand that when profound and sustained empathy is extended by one person to another person, much healing of the inevitable human woundedness that takes place over the course of a life can be accomplished. This is akin to what the social psychologist Una McCluskey has suggested in her "Adult Attachment and Exploratory Interest-Sharing Theory": a person who does not have the lived experience of empathy will rarely be able to trust that seeking care and support is a viable option in situations of anxiety and emotional upheaval.[30]

Angela's emotionally warm salutation has the power to counter movements of isolation among the companions, whereby the members

26. Bornstein and Rusconi, *Women and Religion in Medieval and Renaissance Italy*, 307. The 1563 Tridentine decree endorsed the 1298 bull of Boniface VIII, *Periculoso* and the Council of Trent legislated that only cloistered life constituted a valid form of religious life for women.

27. Makovski, *"A Pernicious Sort of Woman."*

28. The text of the rule that will be used is the edition produced for private circulation by M. Ignatius Stone since it is annotated with verse numbers (Stone, *Commentary on the Writings of Saint Angela Merici*).

29. In her inspirational commentary on the Rule Mary Cabrini Durkin notes that when she addresses the sisters three further times in the Prologue (vv. 7,15, 22) she inverts the usual Italian order of *mie sorelle* so that it becomes the more emphatic and intimate *sorelle mie* (Durkin, *Angela Merici's Journey of the Heart*, 49).

30. McCluskey, *To Be Met as a Person.*

would try to sort their problems on their own. She intuits the central insights that attachment theory has offered to spirituality today in showing the fundamental importance of experiences of warm human companionship, not only for social support and solidarity among the companions, but also for fostering growth in intimacy with God.[31]

The twelve chapters of Angela's *Rule* predominantly deal with practical matters such as admission procedures, religious practices and governance. The inspirational paragraphs are notable for the organizing metaphor used to describe the spirituality of the companions; they are to come to know themselves as "spouses" of Christ. The solitude that they embrace in a spirit of communal warm affection serves to draw them into an experience of God's intimate love. Personal knowledge of the strength of God's affection will give them the resilience necessary to stand against the violence and injustices of the society in which they live, as Judith stood against Holofernes.[32]

In choosing the spousal metaphor to convey the nature of the divine relationship in which Angela's innovative vision for a spiritual community of companions is grounded, Angela is not unique. I already noted in my commentary on Syncletica's life[33] how Syncletica drew on her listeners' knowledge of wedding celebration their society to describe the spiritual relationship in which her circle-of-companions' initiative was grounded. Similarly, in the lives of Moninne of Kileevy[34] and Mary of Oignies[35] a nuptial metaphor is employed to convey the depth and strength of the divine bond from which their religious inspiration flows. As previously noted the eminent Irish spirituality scholar Jack Finnegan has written elegantly of the profound significance of metaphor in spiritual classics:

> Metaphor is a privileged locus of spiritual energy and its figurative expression: it helps us engage with and say the unsayable. Metaphors help us to glimpse the profundity of life, catch glints of the Spirit, sense the building wave of soul . . . metaphors help us speak about those thin places where the sacred hovers tantalisingly just beyond our fingertips.[36]

31. Granqvist, "On the Relation between Secular and Divine Relationships," 1–18.

32. Prologue, Verse 30.

33. See pp. 46–54 above.

34. *Life,* par. 15.

35. Ibid., par. 88.

36. Finnegan, *The Audacity of Spirit,* 119.

Something more significant than an historical coincidence is occurring then when we observe that the women spiritual entrepreneurs being considered here each turn to marriage to describe the foundations of their spiritual initiatives. Instead, the commonality of metaphor highlights the mystical foundations of the new spiritual pathway being forged by each woman. Each one's initiative flows from a level of her personality, which goes beyond what is accessible through her ordinary capacities of attentiveness, knowing, and choosing. Recently Beverly Lanzetta has drawn attention to the intrinsic capacity that mystical consciousness possesses to impel "contemplative ethics."[37] Those who follow the leading of God's love into intimate encounter develop "a specific ethical consciousness—an ethics of perfection—that emphasizes the attainment of deification, and is closely associated with the nascent monastic communities."[38]

No accidental connection exists then between love mysticism and the compelling impulse experienced by Angela to carve out space in her society for those who shared the common longing to journey into intimacy with God. In her helpful analysis of the significance of bridal spirituality, Hildegard Elisabeth Keller has distinguished between "inside" and "outside" views.[39] All the cases of bridal spirituality being considered here represent "inside" views since they point to original, personal, authentic religious experience. Nevertheless all contemporary interpretation of the bridal metaphor, as used in the lives of women here being retrieved, must take account of the fact that the historically conditioned form of the marriage relationship in the societies in which the metaphor is used overshadows its usage. At the same time it must be acknowledged that the Song of Solomon clearly shines through as an "outside" resource providing transhistorical "existential and literary inspiration."[40] Thus Keller acknowledges that "erotic formulas . . . make it possible to articulate things that scarcely could be spoke about except in metaphor, for example, . . . individual experiences of God."[41]

Therefore, as is the case with all metaphors, the image of the bride of Christ points beyond itself. It depicts a human being exceptionally sensitive to the contours of God's manifestations: God's guiding voice in

---

37. Lanzetta, "Contemplative Ethics," 1–18.

38. Ibid. 2.

39. Keller, *My Secret Is Mine*, 44–62.

40. Ibid., 49.

41. Ibid., 265.

the cacophony of competing advisors; God's healing voice in times of wounding; God's intimate, loving word in the deep recesses of the human soul. As spousal bonds generate deep interpersonal attunement over the passage of time, so Angela and the other women mystics considered here point to the profound levels of emotion, knowledge, and insight into which the intentional, committed spiritual seeker is drawn. Very little recent writing on the renewal, refounding, or reimagining of women's religious life has attended to the mystic journey from which deep change emerges. Yet, the pervasiveness of the metaphor of being "spouse of Christ" in all the women we have read here surely points to a foundational source of the radical, singular innovative contribution made by each of them. Here I concur with Beverly Lanzetta's insight in *The Mystic Heart*: "Women's inner life mirrors in certain measure the outer conditions of women's personal and collective health. If this interior level of interpretation is ignored or trivialized, one of the most significant dimensions of effective analysis and social change is overlooked."[42]

Emotional warmth and spousal imagery are complemented by a third distinctive characteristic in the text of Angela's *Rule*. The innovative contribution she made was not dependent solely on her own intuition and spiritual giftedness. She drew deeply from the well of spiritual wisdom available to her. In particular, the frequent inclusion of biblical references and allusions in the inspirational chapters of the text is remarkable—seven of the fourteen sentences of the prologue contain biblical material.[43] In this section of the *Rule* we see that the biblical statements Angela uses are not employed as simple endorsements of the vision she is setting down for those who come after her; instead they serve to counsel, advise, encourage, and challenge. One particularly interesting example is her invitation to live "like Judith bravely cutting off the head of Holofernes." In order to consider the image of Judith that Angela Merici has in mind when she made her exhortation it may be useful to consider the depiction of Judith in Italian art in Angela's time. The most notable artist of the period who created a depiction of Judith slaying Holofernes was Artemitia Gentileschi (1593–1652/1653). She was the daughter of a prominent Roman artist, Orazio Gentileschi, and was one of the first women to achieve recognition in the predominately male world of post-Renaissance art. The depiction of the murder scene in question can be

---

42. Lanzetta, *Radical Wisdom*, 9.

43. Matt 24:13; Luke 11:28; 1 Pet 1:8; Acts 14:22; 2 Cor 1:3; Matt 22:30; Jdt 8:1–15:35. See Stone, *Commentary* 1–13.

seen in the Uffizi Gallery in Florence. Simple details in the picture reveal the strength of intention Judith brings to her renowned act. Her sleeves are rolled up, depicting her premeditated intention to set her face against the brutality of her times. Her signature in the lower right corner reads, *Ego Artemitia. Lomi fec* ("I am Artemitia. I made this"). This strong, bold stance that the remembrance of Judith engenders for Angela Merici also shines through Artemitia's signature. The viewer is challenged by the signature to consider the inner determination shared between the artist and her character, both females undertaking nonconventional actions: the one, murder; the other, depiction of murder.

The invocation of the biblical character of Judith as an inspiration of courage cannot be isolated, however, from Angela's references to others who had gone before her on the journey of faith: Saint Ursula, Blessed Alexander, and Anna (the woman of prayer in the temple from Luke's gospel). Thus, a living sense of the companionship that exists within the communion of saints permeates the *Rule*. The title of her group is the primary symbol of this sensibility: Companions of Saint Ursula. The unique vision that inspired this choice of title is more evident when it is compared with the names of other religious groups coming into being at the same time in Italy: the Theatines,[44] Somaschi,[45] and the Oratorians[46] to mention just a few. Angela's reference to Blessed Alexander has proved more difficult for commentators on the rule to trace[47] but the name seems to be refer to one of seven brothers venerated among early Roman martyrs.[48] The reference to Anna (Luke 2:36–38) is included to illustrate the mutual positive interaction between prayer and fasting. The titular choice made for Angela's followers, and the inclusion of references to a further three lives in the rule, exhibits a sense of the communion of saints that

44. The founder, Gaetano di Tiene, succeeded in securing the support of Peter Caraffa (a bishop of Theate and afterwards cardinal and pope) and made him the first superior of the community, which was named after his diocese in 1524. See Hudon, *Theatine Spirituality*.

45. In 1532 Jerome Emiliani founded a religious society, at Somasca, a north Italian village located between Milan and Bergamo, after which the members became known as Somaschi. See Mullett, *The Catholic Reformation*, 71.

46. The Oratorians were founded by Philip Neri in Rome in 1564. Members commit to stability, which means they are normally committed to belonging to a particular Oratory, for life where they gather for prayer.

47. Stone, *Commentary*, 50; Durkin, *Angela Merici's Journey to the Heart*, 246.

48. Bunson et al., *Our Sunday Visitor's Encyclopedia of Saints*, 746.

Elizabeth Johnson has referred to as the "companions in memory and hope" model.[49] In her account of this model Johnson notes,

> This is a very particular kind of remembering. It does not revisit the past in order to dwell there with nostalgic sentimentality. Rather, it brings the witness of past lives forward into the present as challenge and source of hope. Telling the stories of our forebears, it releases the power of their "lesson of encouragement."[50]

Angela Merici and the Future

The life and rule of Angela Merici provide a unique insight into the journey into solitude required to create a new expression of a life form structured around the spiritual journey. The Merician legacy reveals the interlocking dynamic between the journey of the initiator and the initiative. It highlights the impact of sociocultural realities on the shape and form of an initiative to form spiritual communities in communion. It points to the creative tension that initiators face between settling for the good already being done—the Dominican tertiary movement in Angela's case, and taking an imaginative leap into an intuitively perceived but undefined future. Angela's prayer in her rule is a moving self-review of her own handling of this tension: "I deeply regret that I have been slow to begin to serve your divine Majesty." "This review gives courage to those who today are on an equivalent journey."[51]

49. Johnson, *Truly Our Sister*, 319.

50. Ibid.

51. Stone, *Commentary*.

5

Nano Nagle

Embracing Solitude in Colonized Ireland

ON DECEMBER 21, 2002, the result of the *Sunday Tribune* newspaper's search for the greatest Irish person was announced. Nano Nagle came in first, one of only thirteen women who made the list of one hundred notable people. In doing so she came in ahead of more widely known persons such as the revolutionary leader Michael Collins (second), the 1999 Nobel Peace Prize-winner John Hume (fifth) and the playwright Oscar Wilde (fifteenth). Many features of Nagle's life as a faith-inspired activist on behalf of the poor are worthy of reflection in the task of constructing a contemporary understanding of women who singularly carve out new modes of living the spiritual journey on the basis of following the enlightenment gained in solitude and stillness.

I believe that the mode in which she embraced mystical solitude has not received sufficient attention in the documentation that gives an account of her life and legacy. Indeed the challenge that accounts of the life of Nano Nagle put before those who read them today is how to acquire her type of imagination, a forward-looking constructive capacity that enabled her, through trial and error, to develop a movement of spiritually inspired women for which no prior template existed. Recently, it was interesting to discover that in the historical overview of monasticism "outside the cloister" created by Anthony Grimley and Jonathan Wooding, Nano Nagle's initiative is the first on a list that includes Taizé, Friendship House, the Iona Community, Rutba House, the Finkenwalde Project, and the Northumbria Community.[1]

---

1. Grimley and Wooding, *Living the Hours*, 34–43.

Two streams flow together to influence the manner and form of Nano Nagle's journey into flourishing solitude. First, the historical period into which she was born was shaped by seventeenth-century royal politics in England. In 1685 James II, a Roman Catholic, became king of England and Ireland, and he enacted a pro-Catholic social policy, which was significant for the Irish populace. He was deposed from the throne three years later. The Irish wished to rebel against this deposition and invited the ousted king to lead them. James borrowed troops from France and landed in Ireland in 1689. In June 1690 his successor and opponent, the Protestant William III of England, landed in Ireland and defeated James on the banks of the River Boyne, North of Dublin on July 11, 1690. James fled to France to his benefactor and cousin, Louis XIV. Eventually this defeat led in 1695 to the beginning of penal legislation against the Irish Catholics through which a series of acts were passed that forbade Irish Catholics from practicing their faith. These acts included the suppression of Catholic schools and the expulsion of Catholic priests.

These historical events were not remote or abstract for Nano Nagle's family as they had been intimately involved in the drama surrounding them. First, an uncle of Nano's father, Richard Nagle, had been secretary of war under James II and so fled with him to France after the battle. He took up residence with James on the royal estate Saint-Germain-en-Laye, west of Paris. Second, Richard went on to have twelve children in Saint-Germain-en-Laye, and so Nano gained a wide circle of second cousins associated with the royal household in France with whom she would socialize when she later traveled to mainland Europe to be educated. The cousins who grew up on the estate at Saint-Germain-en-Laye attended a school there of the Sisters of St Thomas of Villanova. Later when Nano was considering a rule of life for the her own spiritual community, she considered the rule of this group.

Nano's Life (1718–1784)

Nano Nagle spent her childhood in a setting of great natural beauty in the south of Ireland on the banks of the Blackwater River.[2] She was born in 1718 into a Catholic family that knew the real possibility of being dispos-

2. The lands on which Nano Nagle grew up are preserved today by the religious congregation she founded, the Presentation sisters: http://www.nanonaglebirthplace .ie/.

sessed of all that had been their home and heritage for more than four hundred years, due to the prevailing Penal Laws.[3] She was the eldest child and had two brothers and four sisters. Research suggests that "there could be a tendency for parents to invest more time and energy in their eldest child, in part because . . . parents tend to see more of themselves in their first child and therefore project their own aspirations on to them."[4]

From her childhood Nano learned the great hunger for education that all Irish people shared. With the suppression of formal educational systems for Catholics, Nano's early education, like that of her contemporaries, would have to depend on whatever could be provided by itinerant teachers. Hedge schools, as these free standing teaching and learning arrangements were called, were independent of Church and state and depended on the resources of parents to recruit and pay[5] teachers. The basics of mathematics, English, Irish, and the classics were usually covered. In dry weather the mobile teaching arrangements could take place outdoors, while in wetter weather kitchens, barns, or ruined buildings were a more viable option. Greg Koos, executive director of the McLean County Museum of History in Bloomington, Indiana, has traced the development of vernacular education in the United States frontier states back to Irish hedge schoolmasters who emigrated from the terrible conditions in which they practiced their craft. Koos has noted that Abraham Lincoln's first schoolmaster was such an Irishman by the name of Zachariah Riney.[6]

As her teenage years approached, Nano's parents made arrangements for her to move forward from hedge-school educational arrangements by the only means possible. Following a strong family tradition, she took a boat to mainland of Europe. The impact of this journey was to reverberate throughout her life. Her convent education in France brought her into contact with a tradition of enterprising women who combined spiritual commitment with subversive social action. Benedictine communities of that era in France and Belgium had many Irish members

---

3. The Penal Laws date from 1695 and were not repealed in their entirety until Catholic emancipation in 1829. They were aimed at the dissolution of Catholicism in Ireland. Their effect is evident in the fact that in 1641 Catholics owned 60 percent of land in Ireland, but that by 1776 Catholic land ownership in Ireland stood at only 5 percent. See McGrath "Securing the Protestant Interest," 25–46.

4. Paton, "First-born children 'pressurised more to succeed at school.'"

5. McManus, *The Irish Hedge School and Its Books.*

6. Hoos, "The Irish Hedge Schoolmaster in the American Backcountry," 9–26.

who had firsthand experience of the social oppression in their country of origin and whose social location in a religious community gave them unique opportunities to empower a generation of women to make plans to creatively resist the social limitations of their surrounding culture.[7]

When she had finished her schooling Nano spent time enjoying an exciting social life in Paris among her extended family and in the company of her sister Ann. This phase of her life was almost ten years long. She greatly enjoyed all the opportunities for parties and entertainment that the Parisian scene presented.[8] She loved the elegant and carefree lifestyle that it was possible to enjoy in Paris.[9] The atmosphere in Paris also enriched Nano in ways that she could not recognize at the time. Among upper-class women active involvement in charity work and spiritual education was prevalent, arising from the inspiration of French figures such as Louise de Marillac, Jeanne de Lestonnac, Anne de Beauvais, Christine Peiron, and Anne de Beaumont.[10] The contrasting lives of rich and poor also came to Nano's attention in her travels around the city. In the later years of her life she recalled how on one occasion, when in the early hours of the morning she was returning in a carriage from a ball with her sister, she caught a glimpse of a cluster of poor people waiting for the doors of a church to open.[11] While this image did not change her life at the time, it slowly released its effects over subsequent years, in conjunction with other life-changing experiences.

Nano Nagle's father died when she was twenty-eight (in 1746), and this change in family circumstances resulted in her return to Ireland with her sister Ann. They came to Dublin, where their mother lived in the north city center on Bachelor's Quay. Here the two sisters tried to recreate much of what they had experienced in Paris, though in different ways. Ann became involved in the type of poverty relief that she would have seen in Paris. This choice created moments of tension with her sister Nano, especially on the occasion when Ann sold a roll of silk that Nano had brought back from France in order to have some fine clothes made in Dublin. Ann disposed of the silk in order to generate funds for medicines for the poor. One milliner who lived in the same part of the city as the

7. Consedine, *Listening Journey*, 11–21; and Nolan, *The Irish Dames of Ypres*.

8. Walsh, *Nano and the Presentation Sisters*, 40.

9. O'Farrell, *Nano Nagle*, 59.

10. Dinan, *Women and Poor Relief in Seventeenth-Century France*; Rapley, *The Dévotes*.

11. Conseidine, *Listening Journey*, 20–21.

Nagles and who would have had the skills to craft Nano's fine cloth was Teresa Mulally. She, like Ann, was busy with initiatives in service of the poor. When Nano's mother died two years later (1748) and Ann died the following year (1749), the involvements of Ann and Teresa seem to have exercised a new influence over Nano Nagle. As Greta Crosby has noted, "Loss makes artists of us all as we weave new patterns in the fabric of our lives."[12] The death in 1753 of Nano's infant nephew, who might have carried forward the Nagle name at the family estate in Ballygriffin, and the passing away of a second sister, Catherine, in 1754 inevitably raised profound existential questions for Nano regarding the purpose of life.

A spirituality born from intense immersion in social struggles was the characteristic spirituality of several women who lived in Ireland at the time of, or subsequent to, Nano Nagle. In Dublin Teresa Mulally, the milliner mentioned earlier, whose fortunes were changed by a lottery win, in collaboration with James Mulcaile, a local priest who had been a Jesuit in France before the suppression of the Society of Jesus in that country, labored in a derelict Dublin inner-city area known as George's Hill. They struggled for liberation from the bondage imposed by illiteracy and poverty by establishing schools. The innovative, religiously motivated responses of other women like Catherine McAuley, Mary Aikenhead, Margaret Aylward, Frances Ball, and Margaret Anne Cusack found outward expression in home visitation, health-care services, orphanages, refuges, and many other initiatives. The socioreligious enterprises of most of these women eventually became institutionalized in convents, though women like Catherine McAuley have left records of the fact that it was never her intention to found a convent but simply to do as the gospel required.[13] The blend of having the opportunity to use traditional domestic female skills of education and healthcare in a public context in response to religious ideals was not confined in its attractiveness to Catholic religious foundresses. Maria Luddy's research on women and philanthropy in nineteenth-century Ireland documents the great numbers of laywomen of different Christian denominations who were taken up in this movement.[14]

All this serves to highlight the fact that the structural expression of the spiritual sensibility of any era is intimately enmeshed with the

12. Crosby, *Tree and Jubilee*, 35.

13. See http://www.academy.vic.edu.au/faith-and-mission/dsp-default.cfm?load ref=31/.

14. Luddy, *Women and Philanthropy in Nineteenth-Century Ireland.*

conditions of its sociohistorical realities. Contemporary feminist analysis of the nineteenth-century women philanthropist's textual representation of their work by the researcher Kathryn Longden has highlighted how these activities provided women with the rare experience of acceptable, autonomous lives in the public sphere.[15] This acceptability was not of course universal, and women like Nano Nagle were, her contemporaneous biographer Bishop Coppinger reports, sometimes bitterly reviled. The effective fusion of a form of spiritual sensibility with the changing aspirations of women in the nineteenth century naturally raises the question of how such a synergy might take shape today.

Weaving the First Threads

After the loss of her mother and sister Ann, Nano Nagle left Dublin and moved to live with her brother David and his wife on the family's rural estate in Balygriffin, the tranquillity of which facilitated a new sense of the direction her life might take to slowly emerge. Nano Nagle began by setting about giving expression to the social compassion and concern that was gradually taking root in her heart. She saw the gospel-like scenes of illness, hunger, and misery in the lives of the tenants on the Nagle family estate. In response she soon followed the familiar spiritual path of her day and traveled to a convent in continental Europe where she could intercede for the alleviation of the terrible suffering she beheld. Her society and family offered her this model of response,[16] and so it was a choice she made intuitively. In Ireland there had been a long tradition of "white martyrdom," of leaving home and family in response to the call of the gospel. While her ancestors had traveled as far north as Greenland and east to Jerusalem and Kiev on their prayer journeys, she went to Europe, into a form of religious life that would been familiar to her from her days in boarding school and from family relations.

However, Nano's choice did not bring her the spiritual consolation and assurances it offered to her ancestors. Turmoil erupted in her inner self. Her sleep was disturbed with voices and images of those she had left behind in Ireland. She had the courage to speak of this disturbance to the Jesuit spiritual director who served the community in which she lived, and the wisdom to act on the advice that she was offered: to return to

---

15. Longden, "Iron Fist Beneath a Velvet Glove."
16. Burke, "Nano and Her Relatives in Religious Life."

Ireland. It would be easy to underestimate the challenges that this decision posed. She was the inheritor of a tradition of social concern that
had given emphasis to Jesus's withdrawing to lonely places in order to
struggle with the social manifestation of evil. In her leaving the convent
she had joined, the fusion she aimed to achieve of two key strands in her
life—a lively attentiveness to divine energy flowing through her and a
deep compassion for the poor—were being ripped asunder. How would
it be possible for her to weave them back together again? The effort to
weave her social concern and her soul journey back together in a new
spiritual synthesis, a new monasticism neither Celtic nor continental in
its form, was her lifetime's task. It was a challenge that led her up many
cul-de-sacs. At first she did not entertain the task of reuniting the two
strands in her own life. When she returned to Ireland from her time in
the convent, she was invited by her brother David and his wife, Ann, to
live with them at their new address in the city of Cork. Soon the voices
she had heard in her dreams, began to call her from the streets and alleyways as she traveled around Cork on her daily business.

She did not immediately entertain the idea of taking a personal initiative to formally establish her form of response to needs of the city, and
she left it to others, particularly to the Ursulines, to carry her vision forward. As she approached fifty years of age, she recruited four Irish wom-
en from her own networks of family and social acquaintances—Eleanor
Fitzsimons (age thirty-one), Mary Kavanagh (age twenty-nine), Margaret
Nagle (age twenty-six) and Elizabeth Coppinger (age nineteen)—to train
with the Ursulines at Rue St Jacques in Paris for the establishment of a
house of that order in Ireland so as to give stability to her social outreach
into the future. When these four women returned to Ireland in 1771 to
take possession of the convent she had built for them, amidst great con-
troversy, she faced the pain of discovering that the structures of Ursuline
spiritual living, particularly the requirement of enclosure, meant that
the challenges of walking the streets to schoolrooms around the city of
Cork lay outside the tent of holy living. Such was her conviction of the
necessity for an evolutionary leap in the form of faith-based expression
of social concern that at fifty-three years of age she eventually decided to
go about giving it a form according to her own insights.

Parallel to the efforts Nano was making to design a structure of faith-
inspired communal response to the absence of educational opportunities

for the people of Ireland, she had also been making decisions about the form and style of her personal way of life. Some time around 1762,[17] when her brothers David and Joseph both made their permanent residence in Bath in England, she moved from the comfortable suburbs of Cork City, where she had for so long resided with David and Ann, to an inner-city cottage where she would spend the next thirteen years searching, praying, interceding, negotiating, struggling and drawing inspiration from the well of creative solitude. In the account of her life by her definitive biographer, T. J. Walsh, we are told she lived in a small cottage attached to one of her schools. It was on the side of the street and contained three rooms and an attic. Though the Ursulines constantly prevailed on her to abandon her cottage, which was located at the gate-entrance of their convent, she resisted their invitations and nourished instead her creative, imaginative response to the call at work within her. The scholar of Irish women's religious history Rosemary Raughter has noted that the weakness of hierarchical structures within eighteenth-century Catholicism allowed considerable latitude to women who wanted to be entrepreneurial in integrating their spiritual sensibility and social concern.[18]

Nano Nagle's spiritual entrepreneurship was inspired by movements that she had heard of, or encountered, on the European mainland. From 1774 until her death in 1784 Nano Nagle toiled to give expression to her spiritual vision—a community of women with the flexibility and depth of commitment to meet the most pressing needs in the society of their time. After being joined by three other women in 1775—Elizabeth Burke, Mary Fouhy, and Mary Ann Collins—one of her chief preoccupations during the final decade of her life was to create a definitive version of a rule of life for the group.[19] She gave serious consideration to rules drawn up by three different French groups. The first group was a Franciscan Third Order whose members served in hospitals in France and the Netherlands.[20] Their rule of life is marked by the priority it gives to "Du Service Divin"; for members of this group service expressed an invitation

17. O'Farrell, *Nano Nagle (1718–1774) & Francis Moylan (1735–1815)*, 47.

18. Raughter, "A Discreet Benevolence," 465–87.

19. The Curé of St. Sulpice in Paris had written a draft first rule for the establishment of Nano's congregation under the title, *Sisters of Charitable Instruction of the Sacred Hear of Jesus.*

20. See Lemaitre, "Statuts des Religieuses du Tiers Ordre Franciscain Dites Soeurs Grises Hospitalieres (1483)," 713–31.

received personally from God (la grace que Dieu luy donnera).[21] However, when Nano wrote about her impression of the rule to Tereasa Mulally, she noted that its fasting instructions would be too severe for working in Irish conditions.[22]

The second group whose rule was of interest to Nano Nagle was the Hospitallers of St Thomas of Villanova, a group who were on the estate at Saint-Germain-en-Laye, where her cousins lived. The Hospitallers had been founded in the seventeenth century in France by a friar of the Hermits of St Augustine, Ange le Proust.[23] The services that this group of women provided were almost identical to those provided by Nano Nagle. The titular patron, Thomas of Villanova, had been a sixteenth-century Spanish Augustinian friar, who was legendary for his compassion for the poor: "The Bible tells us that the poor, the downtrodden, the oppressed, the needy, and the hungry and thirsty were the Lord's favorites. Why, then, should they not be our favorites as well?"[24]

Nano was unable to obtain a copy of the rule of this group for her perusal because of an internal requirement that it be kept confidential to the group. Through her family circle she was able to obtain a description of its main elements, all of which, she asserted to Teresa Mulally,[25] closely corresponded to the day-to-day-living realities of her group. However, the solemn vows taken by the sisters in the group would require the practice of enclosure, which service of her schools in Cork City could not accommodate.

The third rule that attracted Nano's attention was that of the Sisters of the Holy Infant Jesus, known as the Dames of St Maur, a group founded by Fr Nicholas Barré in France in 1666. Nicholas Barré was a Minim priest who gathered a group of women to work for the education of poor girls in a very effective small school system. Members of the religious group he brought together were free to travel and live in the areas where they worked since they were not confined by the cloister regulations applied by the Ursulines. There are no reflections by Nano Nagle in her letters on the rule of the Sisters of the Holy Infant Jesus.

21. Ibid. 722.

22. Walsh, *Nano Nagle*, 263.

23. Ange le Proust provided a detailed commentary on the Augustinian Rule for the group he founded, *Treatise on the Rule of Saint Augustine*.

24. See http://www.augustinianpress.org/saint-thomas-of-villanova.html/.

25. Walsh, *Nano Nagle*, 263.

The issue of a definitive rule that would capture the inspiration she had embodied over her lifetime was not resolved before she died. In the end the intangible spirit of her life superseded the written description of its direction, and this may be a noteworthy point for new-monasticism leaders today.

Nano Nagle and the Spirit of Her Rule of Life

Because Nano Nagle's legacy is often presented in terms of her innovative social activities, the inner work of embracing transformative solitude, which was the root and foundation of her endeavors, is sometimes marginalized in discussions of her life. This reluctance to discuss the mystical, contemplative energy that unfolded in and through her initiatives may have its origins in the association of spirituality with inner journeys far removed from the back alleyways of cityscapes. For the past century scholars of mysticism have, however, challenged the divorce between contemplative attunement and outer social engagement that has bedeviled much writing in spirituality. Confronted by the reality of lives such as Ignatius Loyola (which, like Nano Nagle's, had a dynamic outward thrust while simultaneously possessing a consciousness of the divine imperative surpassing ordinary awareness), the early twentieth-century spirituality scholar Joseph de Guibert concluded, "we are not here dealing with a mysticism of introversion turned chiefly towards the depth of the soul . . . and a union that is as far removed as possible from all that is perceptible to the senses. Instead we are considering a divine activity which affects the entire person."[26] de Guibert went on to describe this blend of transformative contemplative awareness in the midst to immersion in social service as the "mysticism of service."[27]

Contemplative consciousness-in-action emerges through an organic unfolding process, subtly and amply described in Evelyn Underhill's classic, *Mysticism*.[28] It is a process that begins with a *personal awakening* from a world of bland, generalized awareness of surrounding realities to a more alert perception of the mysterious significance of the events of

26. Guibert, *The Jesuits*, 55.

27. Ibid., 77.

28. Underhill, *Mysticism*. This book has two major sections; the first part reviews "The Mystic Fact" and categories the variety of mystical consciousness while the second part presents "The Mystic Way." This latter section informs the discussion of the mystical dimension of Nano Nagle's legacy.

one's life. As has been seen above, this happened gently and gradually for Nano Nagle through such encounters as her observation from her carriage, when returning from a ball, of poor folks waiting in the early morning for Mass at a Paris church door, the untimely death of her compassionate sister Ann, and the encounter after her bereavements with the profoundly impoverished lives of the families living on the family estate. For Nano Nagle, a central feature of awakening to the mystery at work in life is that the call to a new vision of reality is sounded through the lives of the poor: the poor in Paris first, then the poor of Dublin, and finally the destitute on the family estate in Ballygriffin, Cork.

According to Underhill, the journey into alert consciousness proceeds from awakening to *enacting and simplifying,* with diligence and persistence, the new spiritual awareness within which life is being lived. In Nano Nagle's case, her change in perception of life's purpose was enacted by spending time in a French convent, by opening schools for the poor in Ireland, and eventually by assuming financial responsibility for her vision after the death of her uncle Joseph, her great benefactor. As Underhill remarks, "At last, as it seems suddenly, the moment comes: tottering is over, the muscles have learnt their lesson, they adjust themselves automatically, and the new self finds itself—it knows not how—standing upright and secure."[29]

Gradually, but consistently, the contours of the unique divine call that was calling for attention in the depths of Nano Nagle's being became evident. Pursuit of this call often involved the suffering of misunderstanding and doubt. The schools projects she began to develop in Cork City after leaving convent life exposed her wider family to great dangers. We know that at one point her brother David, with whom she lived "fell into a violent passion and said a vast deal on the bad consequences which may follow."[30] The experience of being at right with one's deepest desires is, however, profoundly empowering and energizing. In Nano Nagle's life the conviction born through encountering tensions overflowed into a multiplication of efforts to establish schools for the maximum number of children—boys and girls. Her clarity of purpose also empowered her to seek to give long-term stability to these works by recruiting a religious congregation to administer them (the Ursulines) and by providing the necessary financial resources to secure this foundation. She experienced

29. Ibid., 24.
30. Letter of Nano Nagle to Eleanor Fitzsimons, 17 July 1769.

the illumination of purpose that those who come through the struggle to be true to the guiding energy of the Spirit know. Her life mood changed to joy and enthusiasm, emotions captured well in a letter of Nano Nagle to Eleanor Fitzsimons (who later became Sr. Angela), the eldest of the Irish group of women training in Paris for the Ursuline foundation in Ireland. She is thrilled that the one of those who will be a companion in her labors, Mary Kavanagh, experiences great depths of spiritual contentment in the her educational endeavors, obviously echoing her own experience: "It gives me vast pleasure to find Miss Kavanagh is so well pleased with teaching in the poor school. It shows a particular call from the great god to take delight in it."[31]

In the classical accounts of the journey of transformation, the pursuit of the still, small voice of the Spirit inevitably leads to a time of impasse and incomprehensible suffering, just as the contours of the journey are becoming familiar.[32] For Nano Nagle this occurred soon after the Ursulines arrived in Cork in 1771, when the inability of the fledgling Ursuline community to take up the care of the schools, as she had hoped, became painfully evident. The Ursuline rule of enclosure was completely incompatible with Nano's best-made plans. Her years of endless investment and careful planning had come to nought. In her enthusiasm, perhaps, she had not noticed the practical impediment to realizing her hopes. Her family, benefactors, and friends would surely have been taken aback by her lack of foresight and her inability to deliver what she had promised. The classical "dark night of the soul" phase of transformative solitude was taking its unique shape within the circumstances of her life.

In recent times Beverly Lanzetta and Constance Fitzgerald have both provided wise and profound analyses of the particular shape that the journey into the impasse experience assumes in the lives of gifted women.[33] They have extended the classical map of the journey into personal authenticity, with its two phases of dark night of the senses (where the person begins to break free from the controlling grip of attachment to comfort and ease) and dark night of the spirit (where the person experiences the disorientation created by a loss of confidence in the natural capacities to plan and deliver life projects) into a third stage where gender-based disorienting dilemmas are experienced. In her efforts to begin

31. Walsh, *Nano Nagle*, 355–56.

32. Sylvester and Klick, *Crucible for Change*.

33. Lanzetta, *Radical Wisdom*, 119–36; Constance FitzGerald, OCD, "Impasse and Dark Night," in *Living with Apocalypse*, 93–116.

again and to find a more effective structure for her vision, Nano Nagle encountered the distinctive pain of being a woman on a journey into God. The description of this phase in the life of Teresa of Avila could well be applied to Nano Nagle: "Her confrontation with her own unworthiness, despair and grief, magnified by the pronouncement of male spiritual directors of her lack of worth, became the medium of her liberation."[34] For Nano Nagle, the negative questioning and distrust of the motives for her constant activities and building programs in Cork City was painful. In a letter sent to her friend Teresa Mulally after a long period of silence, she disclosed the response she saw necessary to disperse the androcentric philosophy of her day, which could not accommodate women moving about without the protection of male companions, and which distorted her good initiatives into salacious undertakings. Nano wrote, "I hope we will show the world that nothing makes us go out only when Charity oblige us."[35] The fallowness of this period of Nano Nagle's life is partly revealed by the unusual gap in correspondence to her enduring source of comfort—Teresa Mulally. The pain and incomprehension of this stage of the journey is often too deep for words.

Moving in rhythm with the music of the Spirit, Nano's consciousness that the purpose of the path she was following lay beyond what she could immediately see became assured and confident. She manifested a unitive consciousness, which, Cynthia Bourgeault notes, "both requires and confers far greater capacities of spiritual attention, surrender, clarity, and equanimity."[36] Fifteen months before her death, in the last of her extant letters, Nano Nagle wrote: "Though you nor I should not live to see it prosper in our time, yet I hope it may prosper hereafter and be of universal service to the Kingdom. I comfort myself with these thoughts when I am most dejected by the many disappointments I have met."[37]

Nano Nagle and the Future

The fact that Nano Nagle died before creating a definitive rule of life that captured her vision may leave a happy space for contemporary developments. Since Ireland today is emerging from one of the most seamlessly

34. Lanzetta, *Radical Wisdom*, 123.
35. Letter of Nano Nagle to Teresa Mulaaly, 24 August 1778.
36. Bourgeault, "Mystical Experience or Unitive Seeing?"
37. Letter 16 in Walsh, *Nano Nagle*, 366.

hegemonic periods for Irish Catholicism, it is inevitable that there is a lack of familiarity with that dynamic spiritual entrepreneurship that characterized the eighteenth and early nineteenth century. The spirit of entrepreneurship has been a key ingredient in recent economic development in Ireland, and this newly developed national trait might be creatively engaged in establishing a new expression of spiritual commitment and socially engaged spirituality, a new monasticism capable of responding innovatively to the existential longings of these times.

6

The Contemporary Turn
to Solitude in Women Writers

THE REDISCOVERY OF THE empowering transformation wrought socially
and personally by time spent in solitude is not occurring solely in the
worlds of monasteries and ashrams. It is widely recognized that the turn
to spiritualities that embrace solitude as a central practice on a personal
spiritual journey, rather than as simply group practice of a religious tradition, is of global dimensions in recent decades. Below I will illustrate
this turn by reflecting on one of the distinctive artifacts of this turn for
women—a wide range of spiritual autobiographies. I will not do this in
the abstract but will proceed instead by considering women's own writings regarding how the turn to solitude as a spiritual practice is working
itself out in their individual lives. Indeed, in a manner similar to a previous era when another upsurge in personal spirituality was democratically
led by the Beguine movement, so today the flourishing of women's own
accounts of the spiritual journey is again notable.

The novelist Flannery O'Connor (1925–1964) has offered important
reflections on how the lives of spiritual entrepreneurs of a previous generation may illuminate a later social milieu. She had a particular interest
in the spiritual seekers of the Egyptian desert. In her view, there was a
strong parallel between the type of "dark night of the soul" shared by
society in the early Christian era, and contemporary times. And just as
the early era of Christianity had given rise to figures who sought solitude
in order to plumb the depths of the changing landscape of Christian discipleship, so she saw herself arising in contemporary times as a "hermit

novelist."[1] Indeed one author has described O'Connor as "the Abbess of Andalusia,"[2] Andalusia being an affectionate name for her family farm. O'Connor's reflection on the lessons in the desert tradition for learning to live authentically in the midst of an assault on the senses by life is best set out in her first novel, *Wise Blood*.[3] Her lead character, Hazel Motes, endures the trials and tribulations of a modern seeker in a barren land. His quest reflects all the soulful yearnings of those who cannot confine their quest to the appropriation of inherited traditions but seek instead to invest body, spirit, soul, and mind in addressing the cry of the soul.

Certainly historical precedents are being reflected in the contemporary turn to creating personal narratives of spiritual unfolding, but the current tide of texts of spiritual autobiography also reveals unique narratives of contemporary spirituality.[4] With the postmodern deconstruction of metanarrative, personal narratives have assumed greater significance. Individual narratives provide inspiration and guidance for those who undertake the spiritual journey today. Since the journey is being undertaken in a great diversity of settings, such as the workplace, the counselling room, the marketplace, and the family living room, there is demand for narratives that tell stories of authentic spiritual seeking in manifold forms. As spiritual autobiographies by women emerge from these new settings, more are encouraged to tell their personal stories of authentic spiritual unfolding through returning to the hearth of being in God.

One narrative of this genre that has been widely distributed is Elizabeth Gilbert's popular film-novel, *Eat, Pray, Love*. It presents in contemporary idiom the inner journey precipitated in Elizabeth when she confronted the profound meaninglessness that assaulted her life. In a manner that is iconic of the spiritual quest of a generation of women who today have incredibly busy lives, she cried out with the fervor of a contemporary psalmist on her bathroom floor in the middle of the night. Considering this incident in her life in retrospect, she realized:

> this little episode had all the hallmarks of a typical Christian conversion experience—the dark night of the soul, the call for

1. O'Connor, *The Habit of Being*, 227. See an exploration of this theme in her writings in Giannone, *Flannery O'Connor: Hermit Novelist*.

2. Murray, *The Abbess of Andalusia*.

3. O'Connor, *Wise Blood*.

4. Ruffing, *To Tell the Sacred Tale*.

help, the responding voice, the sense of transformation. But I
would not say that this was a religious conversion for me, not in
that traditional manner of being born again or saved. Instead,
I would call what happened that night the beginning of a religious conversation. The first words of an open and exploratory
dialogue that would, ultimately, bring me very close to God,
indeed.[5]

The ancient theme of pilgrimage, in a new manifestation, fills the
remaining chapters of the autobiography: a pilgrimage to Italy (where
Gilbert learns to Eat), to India (where she learns to Pray), and Thailand
(where she learns to Love). The story tells how Gilbert leaves her everyday involvements and sets off on pilgrimage so as to learn more about
the conversion calling out to her for attention. She follows a three-phase
path. First, she leaves her familiar and hectic schedule, with its highly
programmed agenda. By immersing herself in the Italian appreciation
of life, she allows dimensions of herself that have been anaesthetized to
come to life. Her appropriation of new values is signified in the weight
that she allows herself to gain during this time. Having been liberated in
her body from cultural orthodoxies about female appearance, she then
moves to India to spend time with a spiritual guide, in the company of
other spiritual seekers. Here she willingly learns to embrace practices
that are characteristic of living with a more alert spiritual consciousness.
She likens her efforts to give an account of her encounter with divine
mystery with the efforts of Teresa of Avila, Rumi, and Hafiz. In doing this
she breaks through a barrier that divides mystics from contemporary,
everyday people. Her description of awakening to mystical consciousness
invites contemporary women readers to consider their own alertness to
the divine.

> Simply put, I got pulled through the wormhole of the Absolute,
> and in that rush I suddenly understood the workings of the uni-
> verse completely . . . I was inside God. But not in a gross, physi-
> cal way—not like I was Liz Gilbert stuck inside a chunk of God's
> thigh muscle . . . ("All Know that the drop merges into the ocean,
> but few know that the ocean merges into the drop" wrote the
> sage Kabir—and I can personally attest now that this is true.)[6]

5. Gilbert, *Eat, Pray, Love*, 17.

6. Ibid., 209.

Something of the same utterly unexpected character of awakening to the hidden and unknown dimension of the spiritual core of the person is evident in the story of Jill Bolte Taylor, as told in her autobiography, *My Stroke of Insight*.[7] Jill was a brilliant neuro-anatomist. However, at the age of thirty-seven she suffered a disabling stroke when a blood vessel in her left brain burst. This resulted in significant loss of her ability (based in the left brain) to speak and to understand speech. While her left-brain analytical functions closed down, her right-brain functions survived intact. Her book describes how her right-brain, intuitive way of processing information awakened her to a mystical perception of reality. Her recovery brought her on a journey into a new way of being in daily life and to the discovery of the importance of the practice of presence in particular: "If I want to retain my inner peace, I must be willing to consistently and persistently tend the garden of my mind moment by moment, and be willing to make the decision a thousand times a day."[8]

In less dramatic circumstances other contemporary women have experienced the global rising of a new spiritual consciousness. Diane Perry, for example, lived a very ordinary life as the daughter of a fishmonger in the East End of London (1943–1961). She and her brother were brought up by their mother, a spiritualist, after their father died when she was two. At eighteen her intuitive attraction to learning more about living with pure simplicity was fanned into a flame when she read, during an airport delay, a book by John Walters—with a Buddha on the cover—that was titled *Mind Unshaken*.[9] The title attracted her because she had found living in the middle of the city a busy and crowded experience, one where she had been exploring implicitly how to live with a "mind unshaken" in the hustle and bustle of daily life.

Today Diane Perry is more commonly known by her Tibetan name, Tenzin Palmo. Her personal journey from London denizen to Buddhist nun has been inspiringly told in her biography, *Cave in the Snow*.[10] After her awakening in the airport waiting area, Diane felt she needed to find a personal mentor so as to grow in an attitude of unshaken mindfulness. In 1960s London it was not easy to find such a mentor, so she concluded that it would be necessary spend some time in India. After staying in

---

7. Taylor, *My Stroke of Insight*.

8. Ibid., 154.

9. Walters, *Mind Unshaken*.

10. Mackenzie, *Cave in the Snow*.

her library job for long enough to put together some savings, she made her way at the age of twenty to India. Eventually she moved to the area northeast of India, and there, in Tibet, she met her dreamed-for guru in the person of the eighth Khamtrul Rinpoche. Having studied with her guru for six years, she became one of the first few Westerners to be ordained a Tibetan Buddhist nun. She then moved to a small monastery in the Tibetan Himalayan valley of Lahaul for more intensive practice. After a while, this intensive practice led her to the decision to seek more seclusion in a small cave in the Himalayas, where she stayed for twelve years, the last three in strict retreat.

In this isolated spot she inevitably faced a diversity of challenges ranging from plummeting winter temperatures to melting ice floods in spring and attendant rockfalls. In all this she almost died twice. Her routine involved meditating twelve hours each day; taking care of the daily chores of survival; giving lots of time to reading, painting, and calligraphy; replying to her large volume of mail; and sleeping for three hours each night while sitting upright in a meditation box. The core purpose of this intensive practice was "to become a quantum physicist of inner reality."[11] In other words, she believed that a person is called to live beyond the isolated self, which is created by an imprisoned solitary ego, and to embrace all living reality. For Tenzin, this attitude was very simple, and it was eminently depicted for her in Thérèse of Lisieux's image of the little flower growing by the wayside, unnoticed but beautiful in itself.[12]

When in 1988 Tenzin Palmo finally came out of her retreat unexpectedly because of visa problems, she felt drawn to reconnect with Western culture.[13] Initially she chose Assisi in Italy as the location to start exploring founding a nunnery that would take the spiritual education of Buddhist women seriously, in line with the dream her guru had encouraged her to develop. However, it wasn't until she returned from Italy to India to attend the first Western Buddhist conference in 1993[14] that she began the project which aimed to contest the lingering view that it was not possible achieve enlightenment in a female body. She founded the Dongyu Gatsal Ling Nunnery with a focus on giving spiritual education and training opportunities to women from Tibet and the Himalayan bor-

11. Ibid., 115. Tenzin Palmo attributes this phrase to Dr. Robert Thurman, a professor of Indo-Tibetan studies at Columbia University.

12. Mackenzie, *Cave in the Snow,* 122.

13. Ibid., 145.

14. Ibid., 153.

der regions.[15] In her view it takes fifteen to twenty years of meditation retreats, usually alone, to achieve monastic Togdenma ("realized one"). This extended training would be the foundation for building a pool of qualified female meditation teachers in the Tibetan tradition. In her journey Tenzin Palmo illustrates one key aspect of the turn in women's spirituality; women are seeking to train as spiritual teachers today and wish to have women spiritual teachers available to them.

The emergence of women as spiritual teachers is not solely confined to monastic settings however. Sr. Elaine MacInnes is a spiritual teacher[16] who works in an environment that contrasts enormously with the solitude and peace of the foothills of the Himalayas. Her spiritual journey has unfolded in the context of prisons. Elaine grew up in New Brunswick, one of Canada's three Maritime provinces, and joined in 1953 a fledgling Canadian Catholic religious congregation, Our Lady's Missionaries. In 1961 her first missionary assignment took her to Japan. Influenced by her a reading of Francis Xavier's biography earlier in life, she had an appreciation of the Japanese spirit, and she eventually went to live with an order of Rinzai Buddhist nuns at Enkoji in Kyoto for eight years. She then moved to the Sanbo Kyodan order, which had a more specific focus on spiritual practice in daily life, in contrast to the other two schools of Rinzai and Sōtō Zen, which focused more on training for temple services. In 1980 she became a Roshi (old teacher) in the Sanbo Kyodan group.

During her training in the practices of Zen, Elaine transferred to the Philippines, and there she began teaching what she had learned in Japan. She received a request from Bago Bantay prison in Quezon City, through the prison underground-communication system, indicating that a prisoner there wanted to see her. These were the worst years of the Marcos regime, and the prisoner who requested to see her, Horacio (Boy) Morales, had been a former friend of the Marcos government, but had become an enemy when he joined the underground resistance movement. He longed to recover the inner peace and balance lost as a result of the devastation of his spirit through torture, and he believed, from what he had heard about her classes, that she could help him. She visited him every Friday for four years, despite the personal danger of such an undertaking during the Marcos regime. The positive outcome of these visits gave Elaine a new mission in life: to bring the inner peace evoked

15. Hart, *The Unknown She*, 193–225. Tenzin Palmo's books include *Reflections on a Mountain Lake*; *Three Teachings*; and *Into the Heart of Life*.

16. MacInnes, *Zen Contemplation for Christians*.

by Zen meditation practice to prisoners around the world. Soon eleven more Bago Bantay prisoners were also experiencing the healing power of Zen silence. Since then her life has been devoted to enabling prisoners to become the human beings they are called to be, through bringing them into that silent space in themselves where they can be liberated. Freeing the Human Spirit is a charity founded in 2004 by MacInnes, which today works in twenty-two prisons across her native Canada. Elaine shares the emerging global conviction that everybody has the capacity to be a mystic, and she has led in the way in establishing the truth of this conviction through her work in an environment that would truly test it.[17] Her spiritual autobiography has been captured in the documentary *The Fires That Burn*.[18] The title arises from the assertion she makes in the documentary that "your spirituality is what you do with the fires that burn within."

Prisoners are not alone however in struggling to embrace a spiritual practice that can run counter to the culture of their environment. Professor Claire Wofteich has eloquently articulated the challenges of spiritual practice in the midst of the school run, the piling laundry, and the relentless intrusions of mobile-communication systems.[19] She contends that women's autobiographical writings are privileged resources for providing a window on daily spiritual practice in the lives of women. Women who have written their spiritual autobiographies have noticed, discerned, named, and told the story of their own spiritual awakening and unfolding. Many cross new thresholds in the land of the Spirit on the journeys which they undertake.

Among the writings that Claire commends are those of Kathleen Norris. Norris's style and interests have been compared to those of Thomas Merton and Hildegard of Bingen,[20] but unlike the work of these writers (who were a Cistercian and a Benedictine respectively), Norris's work does not carry the association of a global religious community, which might bring it to wider, international notice. Three of her works are particularly important for women's journeys today. *Dakota: A Spiritual*

---

17. *The Fires That Burn—The Life and Work of Sister Elaine MacInnes* is a one-hour documentary on her life produced by Vision TV in 2005. See http://www.maystreet .ca/portfolio/the-fires-that-burn-the-life-and-work-of-sister-elaine-macinnes/.

18. Production Company: The May Street Group Film, British Columbia, Canada (2005).

19. Wolfteich, "Standing at the Gap," 251–56.

20. Haueisen, *40-Day Journey with Kathleen Norris*, 19.

Geography[21] invites readers to reflect on the portals of mystery within the ordinariness of the space where home is located. For Norris, South Dakota was a place where she had spent many summers with her grandparents. It also became the space within which she and her poet husband lived their creative callings. *Amazing Grace: A Vocabulary of Faith*[22] is a personal exploration of returning to spiritual resources—something Norris had abandoned in early adulthood because of the perception that they were just something for children—and of finding therein sustenance there for living the struggles of adult existence.

Kathleen Norris's *Cloister Walk* is a piece of writing that provides unique assistance to women who wish to be part of the new awakening of spiritual consciousness happening today. The text has the format of a one-year journal, running from September to August. It was written while Kathleen held a residency at St John's Abbey in Collegeville, Minnesota. The liturgical calendar and practices of the abbey provide a framework on which she hangs her thoughts about living with a mindful rhythm. She reflects on the coincidence between the ancient belief in the healing power of chant and the contemporary scientific confirmation of this wisdom.[23] The prophetic power of writing, of giving voice to and providing words for often unspeakable suffering also receives attention in Kathleen's reflections.[24] She questions why the tales of brave women in the Christian tradition, such as the early martyrs—Agnes, Agatha, Barbara, Catherine, Cecilia, Dorothy, Lucy, Margaret, and so on—have been muted so that the power of these stories to inspire women who confront new forms of violence has been neutered. In this view, she is in solidarity with that of the radical feminist Andrea Dworkin, who, reflecting on the sexual exploitation of young women in contemporary culture, has commented that the current exploitation of women extends well beyond the virginal violations of early Christianity and is now "not the blood of the first time" but "the blood of every time."[25]

The Harvard professor of ministry Stephanie Paulsell has also drawn attention to the theme of the body in women's spiritual autobiographies in the past twenty years. She contends that despite the differences in

21. Norris, *Dakota: A Spiritual Geography*.

22. Norris, *Amazing Grace*.

23. Norris, *The Cloister Walk*, 329.

24. Ibid. 214–15.

25. Dworkin, *Intercourse*, 219, quoted in ibid., 200–202.

autobiographical texts, it is possible to detect a common quest among the authors to discern the body as a neglected terrain of spiritual awakening, spiritual insight and spiritual commitment. Paulsell has made her own contribution to this discernment in her publication, *Honoring the Body*. She grounds her discernment in the conviction that bodies are made in the image of God's own goodness and are the dwellings of divine presence. Paulsell writes, "The practice of honoring the body challenges us to remember the sacredness of the body in every moment of our lives."[26] Neglected moments of revelation are drawn to the reader's attention in her hymn to unfolding incarnation. Bathing, for example, is retrieved as a moment of encounter with the compassionate heart of Jesus, who bathed the feet of his friends (John 13). Compassionate touching, is also a gospel act, and the tenderness and care with which the gift of touch is shared in our lives is challenged by the life of Jesus. Adorning the body can be a moment of evocation of the deeper protective presence surrounding us in God. The act of adornment also evokes a connection with the beauty and distinctiveness with which each plant blooms. In her evocative text Paulsell crosses a threshold into the neglected terrain of the body as locus of divine encounter.

In an equivalent manner, the threshold of intimate friendship has receiving focused attention in the spiritual autobiographical writing of Cynthia Bourgeault titled *Love Is Stronger Than Death: The Mystical Union of Two Souls*.[27] The book tells the story of the spiritual partnership between a hermit monk at Snowmass, Colorado, and the author, who was in residence on the monastery grounds. In particular, Bourgeault explores the continuing journey of spiritual and personal transformation with a soul friend beyond the grave, a conviction that she came to hold subsequent to the death of Br. Raphael Robin, her hermit monk-friend. In exploring this journey she draws on interspiritual resources which can enlighten its contours, such as the Sufi tradition of "dying before you die,"[28] a phrase that echoes the teaching of Jesus that "whoever loses his life will find it."[29] While she recognizes the possibility of accusations of subjective bias or narcissism in her narrative, the sincerity with which she presents her experience has its own power to engage the reader.

26. Paulsell, *Honoring the Body*, 6.

27. Bourgeault, *Love Is Stronger Than Death*.

28. Ibid., 106.

29. Matthew 16:25

The selection of writings profiled above also reveals a new turn even *within* women's spirituality. Twenty years ago Carol Christ's *Diving Deep and Surfacing: Women Writers on Spiritual Quest*[30] revealed how the writings of Kate Chopin, Margaret Atwood, Doris Lessing, Adrienne Rich, and Ntozake Shange could inform women's search for spiritual renewal. The current menu of writings are, however, more intimate and less political. They reveal the joys and excitement, the struggles and pain, of those who intentionally and consistently embark on the soul's journey in the deeply ordinary ebb and flow of daily life. In this turn to personal narratives of spiritual unfolding there is an ongoing invitation to each reader to consider how one's own narrative of the journey might be told. They are resources of empowerment and guidance.

A More Intense Solitude

A more intense solitude and distanciation from daily-life intensity is, however characteristic of some other contemporary spiritual writings by women.[31] Karen and Paul Fredette, who live in North Carolina, have over recent years been managing an expanding circulation of the newsletter *Raven's Bread* a quarterly production for those interested in contemporary expressions of intentional solitude. The newsletter derives its name from the experience of Elijah the prophet, in 1 Kings 17:1–6, where a raven, sent by God, carried food to Elijah during his months of solitude at the Wadi Cherith. In 2008 the Fredettes published a thoughtful collection of lessons learned from extensive correspondence, over a twelve-year period, with more than a thousand people exploring modes of intentional silence or solitude of heart, including vowed hermit life. In particular, they report the findings of a survey that they conducted among their newsletter subscribers in 2001. Regarding the gender of those pursuing practices of intentional silence or solitude they found that it was two-to-one female-to-male ratio. This survey finding corresponds to the current ratio in subscribers to the newsletter, thus indicating the particularity of the rise of new-monastic spiritualities among women.

Karen Karper Fredette brings unique experience to analyzing the data, as her life journey may possibly exhibit some stages of evolution in

30. Christ, *Diving Deep and Surfacing.*

31. A less developed version of the material below may be found in Flanagan, "Visionary Women," 73–92.

a new monasticism. Karen was a sister in the Poor Clares of Perpetual Adoration for thirty years. She then lived as a Poor Clare hermit for six years, embracing the solitude of life in Colt Run Holler, West Virginia. After that, she moved to artistic enterprises to a secluded location at 3,400 feet, in the mountains of North Carolina, where she produces designed, quilted wall hangings for homes, sacred places, and workplaces.[32] She married and continued to maintain a contemplative rhythm in the wooded mountain setting with her husband, Paul Fredette. Karen and Paul define themselves as married hermits, and voluntarily limit their social interactions, including living without television or local newspapers. As a couple they have dedicated their lives to solitude and silence, in honor of which they call their hermitage home Still Wood.

Karen Karper has told her story in *Where God Begins to Be: A Woman's Journey into Solitude*.[33] Her autobiography is a contemporary lived expression of a journey similar to that of Syncletica or Moninne. In her Poor Clare community, she came to the point where she could no longer live authentically the spiritual call she experienced. She came to know that she needed to lose all she had become in order to become what the Spirit was calling her to be. She says, "I made this mad leap out of the security of contemplative life in the monastery into solitude, because I sensed that only in solitude would I experience the wildness of the new age being a-borning in the Church."[34] Later in her memoir she clarifies further the purpose of honoring solitude in her life: "As a hermit, I seek solitude, not so much to be alone as to bring together in myself all the disparate strands of life in our world. It is not a work I can do; only the Spirit can accomplish this re-weaving into unity; I am privileged to be part of the loom."[35]

The overlap between Syncletica and Karen in the use of seafaring metaphors to describe the journey on which they set out is noticeable. Karen compares the commitment to live from the inside out as equivalent to embarking on a sea journey in the most challenging circumstances. One sails by night rather than by day, and so it is necessary to become familiar with the guidance offered by nature as made present in the moon and stars. Inner light of the kind experienced by John of the Cross and

---

32. See http://www.creatorsoutlet.com/.

33. Karper, *Where God Begins to Be*.

34. Ibid. 18.

35. Ibid. 71.

articulated in his poem "The Dark Night," where he speaks of no other light to guide him except than the light burning in his heart,[36] is also essential for the journey. The fragility of the vessel in which the journey is undertaken is also deeply experienced—it is a "leaky boat."[37] With the usual barricades to distractions removed from the daily schedule of life, Karen suggests it is inevitable that the defenses against intimate self-knowing are breached. The awareness this generated (that she was collaborating with a power greater than one she could personally create) was humbling, and it became clear to her that it is necessary to befriend the wind, the waves, and the dark, which are the language of the unknowable.

The account of Karen's journey into solitude echoes other classic accounts of contemplative education through immersion in nature. In particular there are resonances in Karper of Annie Dillard's *Pilgrim at Tinker Creek*,[38] an account of eight years of deep observation of Tinker Creek, a natural oasis in a suburban area surrounded by forests, other creeks, mountains, and myriad forms of animal life. Dillard stalks muskrat, and Karper follows deer trails through the woods. For Dillard as narrator, the creek itself is as sacred as a church; it is here that she encounters God's grace in its purest form.

The *Raven's Bread* newsletter has also been very useful in providing narrative accounts of women in a great variety of circumstances who are undertaking the journey into solitude today. A typical example is an obituary from May 13, 1998, in *Raven's Bread* on the death of Cecilia Wilms, a hermit who lived in Our Lady of the City Hermitage in Spokane, Washington. The date of her death and the date of the obituary are the same.[39] Cecilia had been born in 1932 in Ghent, Belgium, and at age twenty-one joined the Cistercian Abbey of Our Lady of Nazareth at Brecht, which has historical associations with the mystic Blessed Beatrijs van Nazareth (1220–1268). When this monastery made the foundation of Redwoods Monastery in California in 1962, Cecilia moved to the United States. Four years later she took a leave of absence and began a new phase in her journey of monastic living. She lived in a poor neighborhood of Spokane close to Gonzaga University, where she was employed part time. Her interpretation of the journey she was traveling has been made avail-

---

36. John of the Cross, "The Dark Night," in *The Poems of St John of the Cross*, 19.

37. Karper, *Where God Begins to Be*, 74.

38. Dillard, *Pilgrim at Tinker Creek*.

39. Weaver, "An American Desert Mother," 3–4.

able in the articles and excerpts from her journal that she published in *Contemplative Review* and other forums. They offer a rich sense of the deeply personal call being enacted by a new monastic—a call into un-mapped territory.

Not all women pursuing intentional solitude come from a back-ground of living formally structured spiritual lives, however. The author Barbara Erakko Taylor, for example, was very much immersed in a thor-oughly contemporary employment arrangement. She had designed an information system for the White House Executive Office and for several Fortune 500 companies. Gradually, however, she began to embrace a life-style that included the intentional practice of solitude and contemplation. This didn't involve her becoming reclusive, but rather she wove her new commitment into her existing routines as a mother, charitable-services volunteer, and friend. Taylor's new contemplative practice gradually transformed her life, and she became the owner of a shop that sells spiri-tual items such as prayer shawls, which are made by women in vulnerable circumstances.[40]

Taylor has described her journey of transformation in two books: *Silence: Making the Journey to Inner Quiet* and *Silent Dweller: Embracing the Solitary Life*.[41] The former is quite eloquent in its description of learn-ing the language of silence:

> In my possessive stalking of silence, I had sought to capture it, ripping it from its source of holiness. But it refused to be en-tombed by me, it withdrew so completely I had no way to follow it. When I gave up hope, *then* it illumined itself . . . *Open your heart,* it seemed to say, *and wait without waiting.*[42]

In diligently following the journey to which she was drawn, Taylor gradually identified core practices that gave shape and structure to her commitment. Her second book provides a description of these prac-tices—silence, solitude, simplicity, solidarity, obedience, and prayer. For her, the integrated living of these practices deepened human authenticity. As she noted, "those who deliberately choose solitude are not posturing as holy people. They are simply trying to recapture true humanity in an increasingly image-driven world."[43] For Taylor, embracing solitude is the

40. See http://www.peaceandprayergifts.com/.

41. Taylor, *Silence*; Taylor, *Silent Dweller: Embracing the Solitary Life*.

42. Taylor, *Silence*, 120

43. Taylor, *Silent Dweller*, 69.

royal road to the utter poverty of the human condition and so leads to the point of utter communion with humanity. This discovery resonates for her[44] with some of the teaching in John of the Cross's *Spiritual Canticle:*

> She lived in solitude,
> And now in solitude has built her nest;
> And now in solitude he guides her,
> He alone, Who also bears
> In solitude the wound of love.[45]

Karen Karper Fredette, Cecilia Wilms, Cynthia Bourgeault, and Barbara Erakko Taylor are just the first four entries in a story of a more intense immersion in solitude by pilgrim women whose lives are rooted in stillness, contemplation, and wonder at the unfolding mystery of God. Many other narratives will be added to the list over time,[46] such as Sara Maitland's exploration of the stages of the journey into solitude in *A Book of Silence;*[47] or Sue Halpern's discussion of the diversity of forms of solitude, chosen and unchosen, in *Migrations to Solitude;*[48] or Annemarie Kidder's portrayal of lived solitude through the centuries and its new manifestations today in *The Power of Solitude: Discovering Your True Self in a World of Nonsense and Noise.*[49]

We have seen above that women today have forged unique, inner-directed personal journeys into the frontiers of spiritual awareness. The shape and form of this movement today may be witnessing to a new movement of transformation by the Spirit, inspired by the type of new imagaination so well articulated by Thomas Merton, who has noted that authentic solitude is not chosen by one's own designs; the call to solitude comes from God and not from trend or custom.[50] The following account of such a call by Beverly Lanzetta enables us to directly encounter this new turn.

---

44. Taylor, *Silence,* 99.

45. John of the Cross "The Spiritual Canticle," stanza 35, from *The Collected Works of St John of the Cross.*

46. Apart from those mentioned in this paragraph, others that might be mentioned are Bourgeault, *Love Is Stronger Than Death;* Pinions, *Wind on the Sand;* Dobisz, *The Wisdom of Solitude;* Ozelsel, *Forty Days.*

47. Maitland, *A Book of Silence.*

48. Halpern, *Migrations to Solitude.*

49. Kidder, *The Power of Solitude.*

50. Adapted from Merton, *Thoughts in Solitude,* 130.

Contemporary Testimony
to Embracing Solitude

Beverly Lanzetta

MY IMMERSION IN GLOBAL contemplative consciousness began over thirty-five years ago when a series of revelatory experiences changed my life and set me on a path of devotion. What I've learned over these years is that the spiritual quest is a fundamental orientation common to the human experience. The commitment to seek God and the pursuit of liberation or union with the Absolute are imprinted in the heart of the world. I also have learned that we live in an era of new visions of the sacred; the monastic heart resides within all people, regardless of life situation or vocation, and it is a sacred duty to share contemporary spiritual ways of being in a world often lacking healthy models of faith.

Youth

I was a solitary child, often choosing to stay home when my parents and sister went out to dinner or to the movies. Alone I felt a Presence that inspired and comforted me in ways that were unavailable with family or with friends. This freedom of being was most apparent in nature, where I formed bonds of intimacy with stately oaks and white-tailed deer.

At five years old I had my first visionary experience. One evening when I was bedridden with the chicken pox, an immense figure of light as tall as the ceiling appeared in the corner of my room. A glowing, pulsating vibration that was wise and calm and protective expanded in the air the way helium fills a birthday balloon. Instantly a sweet feeling of comfort filled my being. The Special One spoke: *You cannot die. You have work to do.* Since my imagination often was populated by spirit figures and intuitive insights, it never occurred to me that others did not see the world the same way.

I remember being a sensitive child. But also wary, a bit traumatized by harsh behaviors and the sloppy manner in which society handled the most significant events. Cruelty among my classmates affected me deeply. Yelling, loud noises, and punishment were unbearable. I learned to withdraw, to pull deeper into silence, to avoid contact, to hide. In a way, I became a critic of the world, interiorized and mute. As I was unable to speak about my secret inner life, my confidence eroded.

Adulthood

Looking back, I recognize elements of the person I am today in that child. I see God working in me, imperceptibly guiding me to a different future. Like many women of my generation, I pursued the path of marriage and children. I needed to sort out the spiritual implications of gender roles: marriage, motherhood, and sexism. I needed to explore a spiritual love that was greater than my individual life and personal pain. I would suffer many trials before I was able to find direction. My understanding of the interior life and the holiness of creation were inchoate until one fateful October day in 1976.

It was on this day that God broke into my world, transforming my whole being and opening me to both the suffering and splendor of reality. I was felled to the ground by the intensity of suffering I witnessed. I was raised up by the transcendent inflow of divine love. Nothing since compares to the awe I experienced and the radical changes that took place within my heart and my soul. While the comprehensiveness of the experience is beyond the scope of this chapter, I can point to three significant aftereffects.

- Human cruelty, suffering, and violence wound the Divine. God bears our suffering. My life must be on the side of mercy and justice. As planetary citizen and as mother, I committed myself to alleviating pain and to resisting the forces of violence and oppression.

- Religious divisions and claims of superior truth, culture, or race violate the universal principle of love. Whoever degrades the circle of belonging harms every being and wounds the divine heart. I committed myself to be a devotee of love, to honor religious diversity, and to never privilege my truth or my religion over another.

- A new vision of the sacred came into the world—one that I associated with the Divine Mother, which I will later name, *via feminina*. This revelatory landscape was spiritually nonviolent, ethically merciful, and theologically open. It heralded a new dimension of spiritual life, perhaps a new way of being human.

Immediately after this series of revelations, I left behind the life I had known. Before long, I was offering classes on contemplation and serving as a spiritual guide to people within and outside religious affiliation. The common denominator in this period was my desire to grow closer to God and to help others embrace the contemplative call. For those who felt disenfranchised by their religion, or who were exploring a renewal of faith, I encouraged them to find God within. Before religion or identity is the mystical capacity intrinsic to personhood. It is the birthright of everyone.

Mystical Dialogue

I returned to academia to pursue a doctorate in historical theology, writing my dissertation on Meister Eckhart's "Desert of the Godhead" or *gotheit*. In Eckhart's mysticism the Desert of the Godhead was beyond the Christian Trinity of Father, Son, and Holy Spirit. Depicted in the Meister's sermons as "neither this nor that," the *gotheit* was the fount of transformation and the renewal of sacred consciousness in the soul.

In Eckhart's divine desert I recognized elements of my own experience. The Meister's dynamic description of the mutual interpenetration of the Trinity and the Godhead, where even God becomes and unbecomes, pointed the way to the intradivine basis for the dialogue of religions. Dialogue among and openness to all religions was built into deep structures of consciousness. Reality was dialogic. God was on the side of openness, freedom. My faith experience outside religion, and faith experiences of others whom I had met or counseled, emerged from the divine nature itself.

Further, in Eckhart's claim that the detached soul breaks through (*durchbruch*) even the highest levels of a religion's metaphysics I found a mystical foundation for the dialogue of religions. At the core of every religion is a metatheology, a nothingness that is overarching of the various particular theologies and religious philosophies. It is also a deconstructive process that prepares the soul to receive the primacy of divine love. Although every religion extols love, an element of tribalism is attached to the claim. Eckhart exhorts the soul to shed self-importance, for detachment is higher than particular love. Detached love is love that ameliorates the suffering caused by false holiness and pride. It promotes an ethic of love for the world, which seeks the spiritual well-being of the whole. It explicitly guards against possessiveness and claims of superiority. It operates on the principle of nonviolence, looking for ways to persuade hearts and minds.

During graduate-school years and after, I was privileged to participate in lively conferences with leading thinkers in the spiritual dialogue of religions, among them Raimon Panikkar, Ewert Cousins, Moshe Idel, Houston Smith, and Krishna Sivaraman. From them I learned it was through the dialogue of religious experience, through sharing of one's faith and mystical apprehension of reality that one entered a point of ultimate depth. Often the deepest sharing took place at times of silence.

Sophia-Wisdom

While my October 1976 experience was implicitly a revelation of the Divine Feminine, it wasn't until I left graduate studies that I realized its explicit call. Kneeling in front of a statue of Mary in the Minnesota woods, suddenly I was overcome with the realization that Sophia was the hidden voice beneath everything. For the first time I understood that her elusive wisdom had been guiding me all along. I decided to read everything I could: the Russian Sophiologists, Thomas Merton's devotion to Sophia in the figure of Proverbs, and female and male mystics who experienced the power of the Divine Feminine.

Sophia freed me from the defense of the separate self. I accepted the path I had been following was an emerging contemplative tradition. Global in orientation, interfaith in spirit, it was a complete spiritual quest, leading the devotee to a God-experience alongside but different from known historical religions. It functioned outside patriarchy. There was no need to reject any authentic faith or diminish ancient truths.

The way of the Divine Feminine is essential to the future of our planet. Sophia's wisdom is silence, because she precedes word and knowledge. Yet she speaks everywhere. She is inexhaustible nothingness, the emptiness of no form. She is the unseen in every presence. She cannot be owned or possessed. It is only through her that the soul returns to its source. The shining face of Mercy, she heals all our sins.

Via Feminina

While teaching a class on the early Christian mystics I coined the term *via feminina*. In describing two Christian paths of union with God—*via positiva* and *via negativa*—I found myself saying there was a third way— the way of the feminine, or the feminine way—*via feminina*. I was immediately struck by the power of the phrase because it evoked the classical spiritual paths and situated the feminine within the lineage of revelation and prophetic history. Within its historical context, the Latin word *via*, meaning "road" or "way," signifies the spiritual journey we take toward union with God. Having chosen the word *feminina*, I wanted to convey a quality of consciousness and a mystical path that include but are not confined to categories of biological sex or attributes of gender construction. The way of the feminine is present in both women and men; nevertheless, I hold that feminine consciousness is embodied and expressed differently in females than in males.

Via feminina represents a spiritual path and a mystical process of inner transformation. As representative of a turn in the mystical path to God, it appropriates and goes beyond the function of the apophatic, or negative, journey as situated within its Western theological context. As a constructed phrase, *via feminina* is related to the spiritual quests and language structures of the classical traditions; but it also disturbs and transgresses them. Standing outside or beyond the logic that formed their language, spirituality, and theology, it mystically functions as a continual unsaying, a continual disruption of the previous thousands of years of saying from patriarchal cultures and religions. Rereading the classical archetype, *via feminina* extends the apophatic process not only to language and conceptual ideas about God but also to the gender disparity codified within its spiritual practices and contemplative paths. It thus involves a radical type of ontological negation that pulls up the roots of misogyny and seeds of oppression that had been handed down from generation to generation and planted in our souls.

Yet *via feminina* is not only a path for women. It has efficacy for anyone who places primary importance on the recognition and elimination of all interlocking forms of oppression. Spiritual liberation today involves an awareness of the interrelationship between embodiment and transcendence that constitutes the whole person. It pays particular attention to integrate the multiple wisdoms of body, psyche, and soul in order to name and heal what offends, diminishes, or violates the person.

Its single most distinguishing feature is that as a spiritual path it does not transcend differences—whether of gender, culture, race, or sex—but enters into them to forge a deeper unity in one's soul and to heal the underlying causes of suffering. Thus *via feminina* is vigilant to the ways the categories that name and define the spiritual life (redemption, salvation, soul, self, God, virtue) as well as the processes or stages of mystical ascent (purgation, dark night, union) repeat subtle forms of gender, racial, or social violence.

The fact that the spiritual journey has been dominated over the centuries by patriarchal thinking, unjust relations, and oppression of women and other outsiders indicates that there is a dimension of the soul that is not free, a place where as a global community we are not yet committed to actualizing the promise of liberation or salvation.

New Landscapes of the Sacred

Global contemplative consciousness and the way of the feminine are intertwined in my work. They reveal previously unseen vistas and distant horizons. They offer hope that a different manner of being, a more holy and sensitive way of doing things is breaking into consciousness.

- These new landscapes of the sacred are premised on the unconditional love radiating from the merciful heart of Reality. If a religion is exclusive, violent, oppressive, or dismissive of the equality of all beings, then it is not a complete spirituality. This is foundation to the divine quest. All must be included in the circle of belong. None left out of the banquet of love.

- These new landscapes of the sacred encourage new sacred expressions, recognizing that there is not one final and only revelation. They foster participation in new faith traditions and are committed to healing old patterns of religious and spiritual thought that promote segregation and violence.

- These new landscapes of the sacred offer a spiritual path for the whole of creation, not only for humans, not only for women. These are spiritual ways of being that take into account the panoply of beings, the cosmic circle, and our more-than-human kin. They thus require an ethic of *amor mundi,* love of the world.

- These new landscapes of the sacred uphold a deeper consciousness of vulnerability, receptivity, and tenderness. They recognize that global contemplative consciousness draws the soul into deeper intimacy with the divine nature, both in suffering and in splendor. It thus requires a new understanding of the spiritual life, of the depth to which the soul identifies with and carries the burden of divine compassion.

- These new landscapes of the sacred are embedded in the world. The mystical force reaches down into the world and emerges up from the earth to protect the dignity of all beings, including the social realities, politics, and religions that serve humanity. The spiritual journey is neither gender neutral nor free from the social impediments of its historical development. The true mystic must be concerned for the whole of creation and work toward its sanctification.

- These new landscapes of the sacred reveal new understandings of the Divine, however named, and are contemporary expressions of Spirit on earth.

Taking a Stand

In 1993 I became an ordained interfaith chaplain. That same year I formed the nonprofit Desert Interfaith Church, followed in 1997 by the formation of the Interfaith Theological Seminary. Both initiatives were motived by a belief that the entire human community is the inheritor of the world's sacred traditions; no one should be excluded from sacramental rites or spiritual practices because he or she has not vowed allegiance to church, mosque, synagogue, or the like; when people of different religious and nonreligious backgrounds join together for prayer and contemplative reflection, a global sign of peace forms.

Holding weekly services at a variety of locations, including private homes and university chapels, our prayer service involved reading spiritual texts and scriptures from the world's religions. Focused around a weekly contemplative theme, the time together was spent in silence, contemplative reflection, and sharing a sacred rite.

The Interfaith Theological Seminary was founded to educate and ordain women and men in interfaith ministry. Committed to spiritual equality of gender and sacramental roles, the Seminary's mission was to minister to all people, promoting peace and healing. Our educational program was two years long and was focused on the contemplative heart of reality. Coursework covered eight areas: monastic and mystical studies, the philosophy and practice of interfaith, the world's religions and sacred texts, spiritual direction, spirituality of nonviolence, new religious paradigms, pastoral theology and ministry, and healing and spirituality. Students were required to complete a social-justice and pastoral-arts internship. The seminary also affiliated with Prescott College, affording students a joint MA and seminary degree.

Returning to Monastic Roots

In all these life changes, the underlying call to solitude and silence never left me. But it was not until I was on a sabbatical that I formally professed monastic vows. The process was assisted and witnessed by a small community of women Benedictine monks. Drawing on the universal call to monasticism, my vows were not made under the auspices of Benedictines or Christianity. Neither were they a rejection of these ancient traditions. Rather, I took vows of commitment to the monastic heart of reality, to that enduring center that precedes religious identification and form. I took vows to love God with everything I've got and to serve others through love.

Taking profession was a transformative spiritual experience. The ceremony itself was simple and beautiful. My consciousness was further re-formed around silence, simplicity, and solitude. Practically, I now assessed everything in my environment from this perspective: what brings me closer to God; what offers peace, great silence? I am certain that the monastic call is intrinsic to all people and is not confined to religious organizations or orders. It is a free call within the self, one that is born with us into the world and to which we owe allegiance. The years I spent avoiding the monk within, too busy with family and work, and perhaps afraid that it would make me more different or too pious, were full of empty concerns. Because there is nothing more natural than to affirm one's monastic nature, living in God's time, seeking transformation into the heart of reality, and loving creation with one's whole soul.

The monastic archetype will take new forms during this century and those to come. The Great Vocation will evolve, as the human heart grows closer to the divine heart.

Schola Divina and the Community
of a New Monastic Way

I am indebted to the world's religions and sacred wisdoms. They have been beacons of light and solace for my soul. Yet, I also have experienced bias, disbelief, disdain, and outright cruelty against myself and other women by the guardians of a particular worldview or orthodoxy. As a spiritual director, I have listened to painful stories of nuns, women clergy, and spiritual women who have been ridiculed, excoriated, and defamed by the power elites within their denominations. Women must rise up and claim their inherent right to speak of God, to speak for God, and to demand the world community foster compassion and love for all the earth's creatures and children. More than ever, I realize that the liberation of women's spirits and the prophetic voice of women are essential to the survival of our planet.

Within the context of my life experience, I formed Schola Divina (Latin, "divine school") as the teaching arm of my work. The name "divine school" signifies that all wisdom comes from God. Under the auspices of Schola Divina, I have offered numerous workshops and retreats on global contemplative spirituality, on new conversations in spiritual direction, on the monk within, and on insight into the path of living for God and in the holy light. As an outgrowth of my commitment to monkhood, I also developed a two-year program of monastic studies, which culminates in participants taking monastic vows.

A remarkable community has formed over the last thirty-five years. Students from my earliest days of teaching have been together for almost thirty-five years. We have formed a stable community, the Community of a New Monastic Way. We have remained faithful to the original vision received in 1976 and continue to explore its many and varied expressions. We have practiced an authentic spiritual path, one open to all religions but centered in the mystical and feminine heart of reality. Despite our members' living around the country, we stay in contact throughout the year via phone and the Internet. We also come together as a group at least once a year for an extended week of study, prayer, and reflection. We envision our work as one of forging a global monastic path, one that honors the contemplative heart of reality and the mercy of nonviolence. Love is always the measure of truth. We frequently discuss the meaning of belonging without boundaries, being committed to our path without being exclusive or superior, and welcoming others to share with us. But more than this, we are bound by our love of the Divine, by seeking total interior transformation to the best of our ability and in the context of our contemporary lives. In this way we aspire to be true monks, mystical monks open to the world.

Bibliography

Abbey of the Arts. Online: http://abbeyofthearts.com/.

Adamnan. *Vita Sancti Columbae*. Edited and translated by William Reeves. Dublin: Dublin University Press 1857.

Adams, Ian. *Cave, Refectory, Road: Monastic Rhythms for Contemporary Living*. London: Canterbury, 2010.

Anderson, Rosemarie. "Nine Psycho-Spiritual Characteristics of Spontaneous and Involuntary Weeping." *Journal of Transpersonal Psychology* 28 (1996) 167–73.

Apffel-Marglin, Frédérique. *Subversive Spiritualities: How Rituals Enact the World*. Oxford Ritual Studies Series. New York: Oxford University Press, 2011.

Ark Community, Northriding, South Africa. Online: http://www.theark-community.org/.

Armstrong, Regis et al., editors. *Francis of Assisi: Early Documents*, vol. 2. 3 vols. The Assisi Compilation 2. New York: New City, 2000.

The Art Monastery Project. Online: http://artmonastery.org/.

Atherton, Mark, editor. *Celts and Christians: New Approaches to the Religious Traditions of Britain and Ireland*. Religion, Culture and Society Series. Cardiff: University of Wales, 2002.

Bagin, Martirij. *Metericon: La Sabiduria de las Madres del Desierto*. Sabidurías 5. Barcelona: Claret, 2008.

Barbour, John. *The Value of Solitude: The Ethics and Spirituality of Aloneness in Autobiography*. Studies in Religion and Culture. Charlottesville: University of Virginia Press, 2004.

Barnhart, Bruno. *The Future of Wisdom: Toward a Rebirth of Sapiential Christianity*. New York: Continuum, 2007.

———. *Second Simplicity: The Inner Shape of Christianity*. New York: Paulist, 1999.

Bandler, Richard, and John Grinder. *The Structure of Magic: A Book about Language and Therapy*. 2 vols. Palo Alto, CA: Science and Behavior Books, 1975.

Beal, John P. et al., editors. *New Commentary on the Code of Canon Law*. New York: Paulist, 2000.

Belisle, Peter-Damian. *The Language of Silence: The Changing Face of Monastic Solitude*. Traditions of Christian Spirituality. London: Darton, Longman & Todd, 2003.

Bell, Catherine. *Ritual Theory, Ritual Practice*. New York: Oxford University Press, 2009.

Bennett, Judith M. et al., editors. *Sisters and Workers in the Middle Ages*. Chicago: University of Chicago Press, 1994.

Beresford-Ellis, Peter. *Celtic Women: Women in Celtic Society and Literature*. Grand Rapids: Eerdmans, 1996.

Bitel, Lisa. *Isle of the Saints: Monastic Settlement and Christian Community in Early Ireland.* Ithaca: Cornell University Press, 1990.

———. "Women's Monastic Enclosures in Early Ireland: A Study of Female Spirituality and Male Monastic Mentalities." *Journal of Medieval History* 12 (1986) 15–36

Black, Christopher F. *Italian Confraternities in the Sixteenth Century.* Rev. ed. Cambridge: Cambridge University Press, 2003.

Boeve, Lieven. *Interrupting Tradition: An Essay on Christian Faith in a Postmodern Context.* Louvain Theological and Pastoral Monographs 30. Louvain: Peeters, 2003.

Bolte-Taylor, Jill. *My Stroke of Insight: A Brain Scientist's Personal Journey.* London: Hodder & Stoughton, 2008.

Bonhoeffer, Dietrich, *The Cost of Discipleship.* Translated by R. H. Fuller. Rev. ed. New York: Macmillan, 1959.

Bornstein, Daniel, and Roberto Rusconi, editors. *Women and Religion in Medieval and Renaissance Italy.* Translated by Margery J. Schneider. Women in Culture and Society. Chicago: University of Chicago Press, 1996

Bourgeault, Cynthia. *Centering Prayer and Inner Awakening.* Cambridge: Cowley, 2004.

———. *Love Is Stronger Than Death: The Mystical Union of Two Souls.* Telephone, TX: Praxis, 2007

———. "Mystical Experience or Unitive Seeing?" December 20, 2009. Online: http://www.spiritualpaths.net/mystical-experience-or-unitive-seeing-by-cynthia-bourgeault/.

———. *The Wisdom Jesus: Transforming Heart and Mind; A New Perspective on Christ and His Message.* Boston: Shambhala, 2008.

Bouwer, Johan, editor. *Spirituality and Meaning in Health Care: A Dutch Contribution to an Ongoing Discussion.* Studies in Spirituality Supplement 17. Leuven: Peeters, 2008.

Boyce-Tillman, June. *Unconventional Wisdom.* Gender, Theology and Spirituality. London: Equinox, 2008.

Brown, Peter. *The Body and Society: Men, Women and Sexual Renunciation in Early Christianity.* London: Faber & Faber, 1991.

———. "The Rise and Function of the Holy Man in Late Antiquity." *Journal of Roman Studies* 61 (1971) 80–101

Brueggemann, Walter. "Trajectories in Old Testament Literature and the Sociology of Ancient Israel." *Journal of Biblical Literature* 98 (1979) 161–85.

Bstan-Dzin-Rgya-Mtsho (Dalai Lama XIV), and Donald S. Lopez. *The Way to Freedom: Core Teachings of Tibetan Buddhism.* New Delhi: HarperCollins, 2000.

Buchanan, Janet. "Monks beyond Monastery Walls: Benedictine Oblation and the Future of Benedictine Spirituality." DMin diss. Graduate Theological Foundation, 1999.

Bunson, Matthew et al., editors. *Our Sunday Visitor's Encyclopedia of Saints.* Rev. ed. Huntington, IN: Our Sunday Visitor, 2003.

Burke, Una, on behalf of the Nano Nagle Commission. "Nano Nagle: Sr St John of God." Online: http://www.presentationsistersunion.org/whereweare/view_article.cfm?id=1165&loadref=168/.

———. "Nano Nagle's Religious Vocation." Online: http://presentationsistersunion.org/whereweare/view_article.cfm?id=1164&loadref=168/.

———. "Nano Nagle and Saint-Denis." Online: http://www.presentationsistersunion. org/news/view_article.cfm?id=1190&loadref=16/.

———. "The Institute of Charitable Instruction of the Sacred Heart of Jesus." Online: http://www.presentationsistersunion.org/news/view_article.cfm?id=1201& loadref=16/.

———. "The Feast of the Sacred Heart of Jesus." Online: http://www.presen-tationsistersunion.org/e-news/100-1d8f9ecb/editions/180-2533a893/ files/301AA0AE-F665-85F2-56DE032201762D5F.doc/.

———. "Nano and Her Relatives in Religious Life." Online: http://www.presen-tationsistersunion.org/news/view_article.cfm?id=1303&loadref=16/.

———. "Nano Nagle's Will and Legatees." Online: http://www.presentationsistersunion. org/whereweare/view_article.cfm?id=1342&loadref=168/.

Burrows, Mark. "'Raiding the Inarticulate': Mysticism, Poetics, and the Unlanguageable." *Spiritus: A Journal of Christian Spirituality* 4/2 (2004) 173–94.

Burton-Christie, Douglas, *The Word in the Desert: Scripture and the Quest for Holiness in Early Christian Monasticism.* New York: Oxford University Press, 1993.

Bynner, Witter, translator. *The Way of Life according to Lao Tzu.* New York: Capricorn, 1962.

Bynum, Caroline Walker. *Holy Feast and Holy Fast: The Religious Significance of Food to Medieval Women.* The New Historicism: Studies in Cutlural Poetics. Berkeley: University of California Press, 1987

Callan, Maeve. "St. Darerca and Her Sister Scholars: Women and Education in Medieval Ireland." *Gender and History* 15/1 (2003) 32–49

Carrette, Jeremy, and Richard King. *Selling Spirituality: The Silent Takeover of Religion.* London: Routledge, 2005.

Cartwright, Jane, editor. *Celtic Hagiography and Saints' Cults.* Cardiff: University of Wales Press, 2003.

Carey, John et al., editors. *Studies in Irish Hagiography: Saints and Scholars.* Dublin: Four Courts, 2001.

Castelli, Elizabeth. "Mortifying the Body, Curing the Soul: Beyond Ascetic Dualism in the Life of Saint Syncletica." *Difference* 4/2 (1992) 134–53.

Céile Dé, Kippen, Scotland. Online: http://www.ceilede.co.uk/.

Chariton, Igumen, compiler. *The Art of Prayer: An Orthodox Anthology.* London: Faber & Faber, 1997

Christ, Carol P. *Diving Deep and Surfacing: Women Writers on Spiritual Quest.* Boston: Beacon, 1980.

Christie, Douglas E. *The Blue Sapphire of the Mind: Notes for a Contemplative Ecology.* New York: Oxford University Press, 2012.

Chryssavgis, John. *In the Heart of the Desert: The Spirituality of the Desert Fathers and Mothers: With a Translation of Abba Zosimas' Reflections.* Treasures of the World's Religions. Library of Perennial Philosophy. Treasures of the World's Religions. Bloomington, IN: World Wisdom Books, 2008.

Clancy, Thomas H. *"The Conversational Word of God": A Commentary on the Doctrine of St Ignatius of Loyola Concerning Spiritual Conversation, with Four Early Jesuit Texts.* Series IV—Study Aids on Jesuit Topics 8. St Louis: The Institute of Jesuit Sources, 1978.

Clay, Rotha Mary. *The Hermits and Anchorites of England.* London: Methuen, 1914.

Cloke, Gillian. *This Female Man of God: Women and Spiritual Power in the Patristic Age, AD 350–450*. London: Routledge, 1995.

Coakley, John Wayland. *Women, Men, and Spiritual Power: Female Saints and Their Male Collaborators*. New York: Columbia University Press, 2005.

Coakley, Sarah. "Is There a Future for Gender and Theology? On Gender, Contemplation and the Systematic Task." *Criterion* 7/1(2009) 2–12.

Coleman, Simon. *Reframing Pilgrimage: Cultures in Motion*. European Association of Social Anthropologists. London: Routledge, 2004.

Collette, Julian. *Emerging Communities, Ancient Roots*. Online: http://emerging-communities.com/.

Community of Aidan and Hilda. Online: http://www.aidanandhilda.org/.

Community of the Mystic Heart. Online: http://www.communityofthe mysticheart.org/.

Consedine, Raphael. *Listening Journey: A Study of the Spirit and Ideals of Nano Nagle and the Presentation Sisters*. Victoria, Australia: Congregation of the Presentation of the Blessed Virgin Mary, 1983.

Contemplative Fire. Online: http://www.contemplativefire.org/

Cooperrider, David L., and Diana Whitney. *Appreciative Inquiry: A Positive Revolution in Change*. San Francisco: Berrett-Koehler, 2005.

Coriden, James A. et al., editors. *The Code of Canon Law: A Text and Commentary*. New York: Paulist, 1985.

Corrigan, Kevin. "Syncletica and Macrina: Two Early Lives of Women Saints." *Vox Benedictana* 6/3 (1989) 241–57.

Cray, Graham et al., editors. *New Monasticism as Fresh Expression of Church*. Ancient Faith, Future Mission. Norwich, UK: Canterbury, 2010.

Croft, Steven, and Ian Mobsby, editors. *Ancient Faith, Future Mission: Fresh Expressions in the Sacramental Tradition*. Norwich, UK: Canterbury, 2009.

————, editors. *Fresh Expressions in the Sacramental Tradition*. Ancient Faith, Future Mission Series. Norwich: Canterbury, 2009.

Crosby, Greta. *Tree and Jubilee: A Book of Meditations*. Boston: Unitarian Universalist Association, 1982.

Cross, Simon. *Totally Devoted: The Challenge of New Monasticism*. Milton Keynes, UK: Authentic Publishing Company, 2010.

De Bhaldraithe, Eoin. "The Three Orders of Irish Saints: New Light from Early Irish Studies." *Milltown Studies* 61(2008) 58–83.

de Gruchy, John W., editor. *Bonhoeffer for a New Day: Theology in a Time of Transition* Grand Rapids: Eerdmans, 1997.

de Paor, Máire, and Liam de Paor. *Early Christian Ireland*. Ancient People and Places 8. London: Thames & Hudson, 1978.

Deresiewicz, William. "The End of Solitude." The Chronicle Review. *Chronicle of Higher Education* 30 January 2009. Online: http://chronicle.com/article/The-End-of-Solitude/3708/.

Dillard, Annie. *Pilgrim at Tinker Creek*. Perennial Modern Classics. San Francisco: HarperSanFrancisco, 2007.

Dinan, Susan. *Women and Poor Relief in Seventeenth-Century France: The Early History of the Daughters of Charity*. Women and Gender in the Early Modern World. Aldershot, UK: Ashgate, 2006.

Dobisz, Jane. *The Wisdom of Solitude: A Zen Retreat in the Woods.* San Francisco: HarperSanFrancisco, 2004.

Doherty, Catherine de Hueck. *Poustinia: Encountering God in Silence, Solitude, and Prayer.* Rev. ed. Combermere, ON: Madonna House, 2000.

Dossey, Larry. *Prayer Is Good Medicine: How to Reap the Healing Benefits of Prayer.* San Francisco: HarperCollins, 1996.

Drane, Oliver. *Spirituality to Go: Rituals and Reflections for Everyday Living.* London: Darton, Longman & Todd, 2006.

Du Boulay, Shirley. *Beyond the Darkness: A Biography of Bede Griffths.* New York: Douleday, 1998.

Duggan, John Francis. "Multireligious Experience and Pluralist Attitude: Raimon Panikkar and His Critics." PhD diss., Toronto School of Theology, 2000.

Durkin, Mary Cabrini. *Angela Merici's Journey of the Heart: The Rule, The Way.* Boulder, CO: Woven Word, 2005

Dworkin, Andrea. *Intercourse.* New York: Free Press, 1987.

Earle, Mary C. *The Desert Mothers: Practical Spiritual Wisdom for Every Day.* London: SPCK, 2007.

———. *The Desert Mothers: Spiritual Practices from the Women of the Wilderness.* New York: Continuum, 2007.

Edwards, Tilden H., editor. *Living with Apocalypse: Spiritual Resources for Social Compassion.* San Francisco: Harper & Row, 1984.

Eggemeier, Matthew, "A Mysticism of Open Eyes: Compassion for a Suffering World and the *Askesis* of Contemplative Prayer." *Spiritus* 12/1(2012) 43–62.

Ellenberger, Henri F. "The Concept of Creative Illness." *Psychoanalytic Review* 55 (1968) 442–56.

Elliott, Dyan. *Proving Woman: Female Spirituality and Inquisitional Culture.* Princeton: Princeton University Press, 2004.

———. *Spiritual Marriage: Sexual Abstinence in Medieval Wedlock.* Princeton: Princeton University Press, 1993.

Elm, Susanna. *"Virgins of God": The Making of Asceticism in Late Antiquity.* Oxford Classical Monographs. Oxford: Clarendon, 1994.

Emmons, Robert A. *Thanks!: How the New Science of Gratitude Can Make you Happier.* Boston: Houghton Mifflin, 2007.

Evagrius, Ponticus. *The Praktikos, Chapters on Prayer.* Translated by John Eudes Bamberger. Cistercian Studies Series 4. Kalamazoo: Cistercian, 1981.

Fedorowicz, Paul. "Everyday Monasticism: The Calling." *Newtimes* 4 (2000).

Fellowship of Solitaries. Online: http://www.solitaries.org.uk/.

Ferguson, Ron. *George McLeod.* Glasgow: Wild Goose Publications, 1990.

Finnegan, Jack. *The Audacity of Spirit: The Meaning and Shaping of Spirituality Today.* Dublin: Veritas, 2008.

Fitz-Gibbon, Jane Hall and Andrew Fitz-Gibbon, *Secular Monasticism: A Journey.* Milton Keynes, UK: XLibris, 2012.

Flanagan, Bernadette. "Sitting Spirituality: Where Church and Seeker Meet." *The Way* 101 (2001) 20–29.

Forman, Mary. "Amma Syncletica: A Spirituality of Experience." *Vox Benedicta* 10/2 (1993) 199–237.

Forman, Mary. *Praying with the Desert Mothers.* Collegeville, MN: Liturgical, 2005.

Foucault, Michel, *The History of Sexuality*. Vol. 2, The *Use of Pleasure*. New York: Vintage, 1990.

Franciscan Order of Céli Dé. Online: http://dfba.home.mindspring.com/celide.html/.

Fraternités monastiques de Jérusalem and Pierre-Marie Delfieux. *A City Not Forsaken: The Jerusalem Community Rule of Life*. Translated by Kathleen England. London: Darton, Longman & Todd, 1983.

Fredette, Paul, and Karen Karper Fredette. *Consider the Ravens: On Contemporary Hermit Life*. Bloomington, IN: iUniverse, 2008.

Frohlich, Mary, "Spiritual Discipline, Discipline of Spirituality: Revisiting Questions of Definition and Method." *Spiritus: A Journal of Christian Spirituality* 1/1 (Spring 2001) 65–78.

Funk, Mary Margaret. *Lectio Matters: Before the Burning Bush; Through the Revelatory Texts of Scripture, Nature and Experience*. London: Continuum, 2010.

Gaucher, Guy. *The Prayers of Saint Thérèse of Lisieux: The Act of Oblation*. Washington DC: ICS Publications, 1997.

Giannone, Richard. *Flannery O'Connor: Hermit Novelist*. Columbia: University of South Carolina Press, 2000.

Gilbert, Elizabeth. *Eat, Pray, Love: One Woman's Search for Everything Across Italy, India and Indonesia*. New York: Penguin, 2006.

Gladwell, Malcolm. *The Tipping Point: How Little Things Can Make a Big Difference*. London: Little Brown, 2000.

Goehring, James. *Ascetics, Society, and the Desert: Studies in Early Egyptian Monasticism*. Studies in Antiquity and Christianity. Harrisburg: Trinity, 1999.

————. "The Encroaching Desert: Literary Production and Ascetic Space in Early Christian Egypt." *Journal of Early Christian Studies* 1/3 (Fall 1993) 281–96

Gonyon, Jeanne M., OCD. *Contemplative Sisters Living Outside the Monastery: A Study for* for the *Association of Contemplative Sisters*. N.p., 1977.

Granqvist, Pehr. "On the Relation between Secular and Divine Relationships: An Emerging Attachment Perspective and a Critique of the Depth Approaches." *International Journal for the Psychology of Religion* 16 (2006) 1–18.

Grant, Robert. *The Way of the Wound: A Spirituality of Trauma and Transformation*. Burlingame: Robert Gran, 1996.

Gratefulnees.org. Online: http://www.gratefulness.org/.

Green Mountain Monastery. Online: http://www.greenmountainmonastery.org/.

Grimley, Anthony, and Jonathan Wooding. *Living the Hours: Monastic Spirituality in Everyday Life*. Norwich: Canterbury, 2010.

Grumett, David. *Teilhard de Chardin: Theology, Humanity and Cosmos*. Studies in Philosophical Theology 29. Leuven: Peeters, 2005.

Grundmann, Herbert. *Religious Movements in the Middle Ages: The Historical Links between Heresy, the Mendicant Orders, and the Women's Religious Movement in the Twelfth and Thirteenth Century, with the Historical Foundation of German Mysticism*. Translated by Steven Rowan. Notre Dame: University of Notre Dame Press, 1996.

Guibert, Joseph de. *The Jesuits: Their Spiritual Doctrine and Practice*. Chicago: Institute of Jesuit Sources, 1964.

Hab Community. Online: http://www.adambucko.com/HAB/.

Halpern, Sue. *Migrations to Solitude: The Quest for Privacy in a Crowded World*. New York: Vintage, 1993.

Harding, Sandra, editor. *The Feminist Standpoint Theory Reader: Intellectual and Political Controversies.* New York: Routledge, 2003.

Harmless, William. *Desert Christians: An Introduction to the Literature of Early Monasticism.* Oxford: Oxford University Press, 2004.

Harrington, Christina. *Women in a Celtic Church: Ireland 450–1150.* Oxford: Oxford University Press, 2002.

Hart, Patrick, editor. *A Monastic Vision for the 21st Century: Where Do We Go from Here?* Monastic Wisdom Series 8. Kalamazoo: Cistercians, 2006.

Hart, Hilary. *The Unknown She: Eight Faces of an Emerging Consciousness.* Inverness, CA: Golden Sufi Center, 2003.

Haueisen, Kathryn. *40-Day Journey with Kathleen Norris.* 40-Day Journey Series. Minneapolis: Augsburg, 2008.

Hauerwas, Stanley. *A Community of Character: Toward a Constructive Christian Social Ethic.* Notre Dame: University of Notre Dame Press, 1981.

Hauerwas, Stanley, and William Willimon *Resident Aliens: A Provocative Christian Assessment of Culture and Ministry for People Who Know that Something is Wrong.* Nashville: Abingdon, 1989.

Hederman, Mark Patrick. *Underground Cathedrals.* Dublin: Columba, 2010

Heelas, Paul et al. *The Spiritual Revolution: Why Religion Is Giving Way to Spirituality.* Religion and Spirituality in the Modern World. Malden, MA: Blackwell, 2005.

Heifetz, Ronald, and Mary Linsky. *Leadership on the Line: Staying Alive through the Dangers of Leading.* Boston: Harvard Business School Press, 2002

Heschel, Abraham Joshua. *God in Search of Man: A Philosophy of Judaism.* New York: Farrar, Straus & Giroux, 1955.

———. *Man Is Not Alone: A Philosophy of Religion.* New York: Farrar, Straus & Giroux, 1951.

———. *The Prophets: Part II.* New York: Harper & Row, 1962.

Hermits of Bethlehem. Online: http://www.bethlehemhermits.org/.

Hesed Community. Online: http://www.hesedcommunity.org/.

Hillesum, Etty. *Etty: The Letters and Diaries of Etty Hillesum 1941–1943.* Complete and unabridged ed. Edited by Klaas Smelik. Translated by Arnold Pomerans. Grand Rapids: Eerdmaans, 2002.

Hoos, Greg. "The Irish Hedge Schoolmaster in the American Backcountry." *New Hibernia Review* 5/2 (2001) 9–26.

Howells, Edward, and Peter Tyler. *Sources of Transformation: Revitalising Christian Spirituality.* New York: Continuum, 2010.

Hudon, William, editor. *Theatine Spirituality: Selected Writings.* The Classics of Western Spirituality. New York: Paulist, 1996.

Hughes, Art, and William Nolan, editors. *Armagh History and Society: Interdisciplinary Essays on the History of an Irish County.* Dublin: Geography Publications, 2001.

Hughes, Kathleen. *Early Christian Ireland: Introduction to the Sources.* The Sources of History: Studies in the Uses of Historical Evidence. London: Hodder & Stoughton, 1972.

Hughes, Kathleen, and Ann Hamlin. *The Modern Traveller to the Early Irish Church.* London: SPCK, 1977.

Integral Monastery. Online: http://www.integralmonastery.com/.

Jamison, Christopher. *Finding Sanctuary: Monastic Steps for Everyday Life.* London: Weidenfeld & Nicholson, 2006.

Janzen, David. *The Intentional Christian Community Handbook for Idealists, Hypocrites, and Wannabe Disciples of Jesus.* Brewster, MA: Paraclete, 2012.

Jantzen, Grace M. *Power, Gender and Christian Mysticism.* Cambridge Studies in Ideology and Religion 8. Cambridge: Cambridge University Press, 1995.

John Paul II, Pope. Apostolic Letter *Novo Millennio Ineunte.* Online: http://www.vatican.va/holy_father/john_paul_ii/apost_letters/documents/hf_jp-ii_apl_20010106_novo-millennio-ineunte_en.html/.

John of the Cross, Saint. *The Collected Works of St. John of the Cross,* Translated by Kieran Kavanaugh, OCD, and Otilio Rodriguez, OCD. Washington DC: ICS Publications, 1991

———. *The Poems of St John of the Cross.* Translated by J. F. Nims. 3rd ed. Chicago: University of Chicago Press, 1989.

Johnson, Elizabeth. *Friends of God and Prophets: A Feminist Theological Reading of the Communion of Saints.* New York: Continuum, 1998.

———. *Truly Our Sister: A Theology of Mary in the Communion of Saints.* New York: Continuum, 2003.

Jones, Alan W. *Soul Making: The Desert Way of Spirituality.* San Francisco: Harper & Row, 1985.

Kaplan, Matt. "When Animals Predict Earthquakes." *New Scientist,* Issue 2591, 17 February 2007.

Karper, Karen. *Where God Begins to Be: A Woman's Journey into Solitude.* New York: iUniverse, 1994.

Keller, David. *Oasis of Wisdom: The Worlds of the Desert Fathers and Mothers.* Collegeville, MN: Liturgical, 2005.

Keller, Hildegard Elisabeth. *My Secret Is Mine: Studies on Religion and Eros in the German Middle Ages.* Studies in Spirituality Supplement 4. Leuven: Peeters, 2000.

Keuss, Jeffrey. "A Spirituality for the Advent City: Thomas Merton's Monasticism without Walls." *Merton Journal* 10/2 (2003) 5–7.

Kidder, Annemarie S. *The Power of Solitude: Discovering Your True Self in a World of Nonsense and Noise.* New York: Crossroad, 2007.

King, Margot H., and Hugh Feiss, translators. *Two Lives of Marie d'Oignies,* by Jacques de Vitry and Thomas de Cantimpré. 4th ed. Peregrina Translations Series 3 & 4. Toronto: Peregrina, 1998.

Klinenberg, Eric. *Going Solo: The Extraordinary Rise and Surprising Appeal of Living Alone.* New York: Penguin, 2012.

Koch, Philip. *Solitude: A Philosophical Encounter.* Chicago: Open Court, 1994.

Koinonia Farm. Online: http://www.koinoniapartners.org/.

Kulzer, Linda, and Roberta Bondi, editors. *Benedict in the World: Portraits of Monastic Oblates.* Collegeville, MN: Liturgical, 2002.

Kruschwitz, Robert, editor. *Monasticism Old and New.* Christian Reflection 36. Waco, TX: Center for Christian Ethics, Baylor University, 2010.

Ladinsky, Daniel, translator. *Love Poems from God. Twelve Sacred Voices from the East and West.* London: Penguin, 2002.

Laird, Martin. *A Sunlit Absence: Silence, Awareness and Contemplation.* New York: Oxford University Press, 2011.

———. *Into the Silent Land: The Practice of Contemplation.* Oxford: Oxford University Press, 2006.

———. "The 'Open Country Whose Name is Prayer': Apophasis, Deconstruction and Contemplative Practice." *Modern Theology* 21/1 (2005) 141–55.

Lakoff, George, and Mark Johnson. *Metaphors We Live By.* Chicago: University of Chicago Press, 1980.

Landron, Olivier. *Communautés Nouvelles.* Paris: Cerf, 2005.

Lane, Belden. *The Solace of Fierce Landscapes: Exploring Desert and Mountain Spirituality.* Oxford: Oxford University Press, 1998.

Lawrence, of the Resurrection, Brother. *The Practice of the Presence of God: The Best Rule of a Holy Life; Being Conversations and Letters of Nicholas Herman, of Lorraine.* Translated by Hannah Whitall Smith. New York: Revell, 2004.

Lanzetta, Beverly. "Contemplative Ethics: Intimacy, *Amor Mundi* and Dignification in Julian of Norwich and Teresa of Avila." *Spiritus* 5/1(2005) 1–18.

———. *Emerging Heart: Global Spirituality and the Sacred.* Minneapolis: Fortress, 2007.

———. *Radical Wisdom: A Feminist Mystical Theology.* Minneapolis: Fortress, 2005.

Ledochowska, Teresa. *Angela Merici and the Company of Saint Ursula.* 2 vols. Rome: Ancora, 1967.

Lemaitre, Henri. "Statuts des Religieuses du Tiers Ordre Franciscain Dites Soeurs Grises Hospitalieres (1483)." *Archivum Franciscanum Historicum* 4 (1913) 713–31.

Le Proust Ange. *Treatise on the Rule of Saint Augustine.* Translated by John Otto. Augustinian Series 24. Villanova, PA: Augustinian Press, 1996

Lindisfarne Community of Ithaca, New York. Online: http://www.icmi.org/home.html.

Little Flowers Community. Online: http://littleflowers.ca/.

Little Portion Hermitage. Online: http://www.littleportion.org/.

LivingStone Monastery. Online: http://www.livingstonemonastery.org/.

Longden, Kathryn. "Iron Fist Beneath a Velvet Glove: Middle-Class Women's Representations of Philanthropic and Voluntary Work amongst the Poor, Working-Class, and Indigenous Peoples in the Nineteenth Century." *Sheffield Hallam Working Papers on the Web I.* Online: http://extra.shu.ac.uk/wpw/femprac/longden.htm/.

Luddy, Maria. *Women and Philanthropy in Nineteenth-Century Ireland.* Cambridge: Cambridge University Press, 1995.

Luibheid, Colm, and Norman Russell, translators. *The Ladder of Divine Ascent,* by Saint John Climacus. The Classics of Western Spirituality. New York: Paulist, 1982.

Lux-Sterritt, Laurence. *Redefining Female Religious Life: French Ursulines and English Ladies in Seventeenth-Century Catholicism.* Catholic Christendom, 1300–1700. Aldershot: Ashgate, 2006.

Maas, Frans. *Spirituality as Insight: Mystical Texts and Theological Reflection.* The Fiery Arrow Collection 6. Leuven: Peeters, 2004.

MacInnes, Elaine. *Zen Contemplation for Christians: A Bridge of Living Water.* Lanham, MD: Rowman & Littlefield, 2003.

MacIntyre, Alasdair C. *After Virtue: A Study in Moral Theory.* 2nd ed. Notre Dame: University of Notre Dame Press, 1984.

Mackenzie, Vicki. *Cave in the Snow: A Western Woman's Quest for Enlightenment.* London: Bloomsbury, 1998.

Macvarish, Jan, "What Is 'the Problem' of Singleness?" *Sociological Research Online,* 11/3 (1996). Online: http://www.socresonline.org.uk/11/3/macvarish.html/.

Main, John. *Monastery without Walls: The Spiritual Letters of John Main.* Edited by Laurence Freeman. Norwich: Canterbury, 2006.

Maitland, Sara. *A Book of Silence*. London: Granta, 2008.

Makovski, Elizabeth. *"A Pernicious Sort of Woman": Quasi-Religious Women and Canon Lawyers in the Later Middle Ages*. Studies in Medieval and Early Modern Canon Law 6. Washington, DC: Catholic University of America Press, 2005.

Malone, Mary T. *Women and Christianity*. Vol. 2, *The Medieval Period AD 1000–1500*. Dublin: Columba, 2001.

Manson, Jamie. "New Monasticism: Envisioning Monks without Borders." Grace on the Margins. National Catholic Reporter, September 20, 2012. Online: http://ncronline.org/blogs/grace-margins/new-monasticism-envisioning-monks-without-borders/.

———. "Spiritual Hunger of Young Adults: Where Does It Come From, and What Might They Need?" Grace on the Margins. *National Catholic Reporter*, September 26, 2012. Online: http://ncronline.org/blogs/grace-margins/spiritual-hunger-young-adults-where-does-it-come-and-what-might-they-need

———. "Two Young Adults Offer a New Take on 'New Monasticism.'" Grace on the Margins. National Catholic Reporter, September 10, 2012. Online: http://ncronline.org/blogs/grace-margins/two-young-adults-offer-new-take-new-monasticism/.

Manss, Virginia, and Mary Frohlich, editors. *The Lay Contemplative: Testimonies, Perspectives, Resources*. Cincinnati: St. Anthony Messenger Press, 2000.

Margoni, Alberto. *Angela Merici: l'intuizione della spiritualità secolare*. Spiritualità e promozione umana 19. Soveria Mannelli: Rubbettino, 2000.

Mariani, Luciana et al. *Angela Merici: Contribution towards a Biography*. Translated by M. Ignatius Stone. Milan: Ancora Milano, 1989.

Mary Clare, Mother. *The Contemplative in the World*. Oxford: SLG Press, 1987.

Maybe Community. Online: http://maybe.org.uk/.

McCluskey, Una. *To Be Met as a Person: The Dynamics of Attachment in Professional Encounters*. London: Karnac, 2005.

McCone, Kim, and Katherine Simms. *Progress in Medieval Irish Studies*. Maynooth: Dept. of Old Irish, St. Patrick's College, 1996.

McDonnell, Ernest W. *The Beguines and Beghards in Medieval Culture with Special Emphasis on the Belgian Scene*. New Brunswick, NJ: Rutgers University Press, 1954.

McGinn, Bernard. *The Flowering of Mysticism: Men and Women in the New Mysticism (1200–1350)*. The Presence of God: A History of Western Christian Mysticism 3. New York: Crossroad, 1998

———. *The Foundations of Mysticism: Origins to the Fifth Century*. The Presence of God: A History of Western Christian Mysticism 1 New York: Crossroad, 1991.

———. *The Growth of Mysticism: Sixth to Twelfth Century*. The Presence of God: A History of Western Christian Mysticism 2. New York: Crossroad, 1994.

———. *The Harvest of Mysticism in Medieval Germany (1300–1500)*. The Presence of God: A History of Western Christian Mysticism 4. New York: Crossroad, 2005.

———. *Meister Eckhart and the Beguine Mystics: Hadewijch of Brabant, Mechthild of Magdeburg, and Marguerite Porete*. New York: Continuum, 1997.

———. *The Varieties of Vernacular Mysticism (1350–1550)*. The Presence of God: A History of Western Christian Mysticism 5. New York: Crossroad, 2012.

McGrath, Charles. "Securing the Protestant Interest: The Origins and Purpose of the Penal Laws of 1695." *Irish Historical Studies* 30/117 (1996) 25–46.

McManus, Antonia. *The Irish Hedge School and Its Books, 1695–1831*. Dublin: Four Courts, 2003.

McNamara, Jo Ann Kay. *Sisters in Arms: Catholic Nuns through Two Millennia*. Cambridge: Harvard University Press, 1998.

Meehan, Bridget Mary, and Regina Madonna Oliver. *Praying with Celtic Holy Women*. Hampshire: Redemptorist Publications, 2003.

Merton, Thomas. *Come to the Mountain: New Ways and Living Traditions in the Monastic Life*. Snowmass, CO: St. Benedict's Cistercian Monastery, 1964.

———. *Conjectures of a Guilty Bystander*. New York: Image, 1989.

———. *Mystics and Zen Masters*. New York: Farrar, Straus & Giroux, 1999.

———. *Thoughts in Solitude*. New York: Dell, 1956.

Mews, Constant J., editor. *Listen Daughter: The Speculum virginium and the Formation of Religious Women in the Middle Ages*. The New Middle Ages. Basingstoke: Palgrave 2001.

Monasteries of the Heart. Online: http://monasteriesoftheheart.org/.

Monastic Interreligious Dialogue. Online: http://www.monasticdialog.com/.

MONOS. Online: http://www.monos.org.uk/.

Moot Community. Online: www.moot.uk.net/.

Morinis, Alan. *Sacred Journeys: The Anthropology of Pilgrimage*. Contributions to the Study of Anthropology 7. Westport, CT: Praeger, 1992.

Morris, Bridget. *St Birgitta of Sweden*. Studies in Medieval Mysticism 1. Woodbridge, Suffolk, UK: Boydell, 1999.

Mulder-Bakker, Anneke B. *Mary of Oignies: Mother of Salvation*. Medieval Women 7. Turnhout: Brepols, 2006.

Mullett, Michael A. *The Catholic Reformation*. London: Routledge, 1999.

Murk-Jansen, Saskia. *Brides in the Desert: The Spirituality of the Beguines*. Traditions of Christian Spirituality. London: Darton, Longman & Todd, 1998

Murray, Lorraine C. *The Abbess of Andalusia: Flannery O'Connor's Spiritual Journey*. Charlotte, NC: St Benedict Press, 2009.

Nano Nagle Birthplace. Online: http://www.nanonaglebirthplace.ie/.

Nehemiah Ministries. Online: http://www.nehemiah-ministries.com/.

Newbigin, Leslie. *The Gospel in a Pluralist Society*. Grand Rapids: Eerdmans, 1986.

New Monasticisms Ireland. Online: http://www.newmonasticismsireland.org/.

New Monasticism Network UK. Online: http://new-monasticism-network.ning.com

Nolan, Patrick. *The Irish Dames of Ypres: Being a History of the Royal Irish Abbey of Ypres Founded A.D. 1665 and Still Flourishing*. New York: Benziger Brothers, 1908

Norris, Kathleen. *Amazing Grace: A Vocabulary of Faith*. New York: Riverhead, 1999.

———. *The Cloister Walk*. New York: Riverhead, 1996.

———. *Dakota: A Spiritual Geography*. New York: Mariner, 2001.

The Northumbria Community. *Celtic Daily Prayer: From the Northumbria Community*. San Francisco: HarperSanFrancisco, 2002.

Nouwen, Henri. *The Way of the Heart: Desert Spirituality and Contemporary Ministry*. New York: Seabury, 1981.

O'Connor, Elizabeth. *Call to Commitment: An Attempt to Embody the Essence of Church*. Washington DC: Servant Leadership, 1994

O'Connor, Flannery. *The Habit of Being: Letters of Flannery O'Connor*. Edited by Sally Fitzgerald. New York: Farrar, Straus & Giroux, 1979.

———. *Wise Blood*. New York: Farrar, Straus & Giroux, 1952.

O'Donohue, John. Online: http://www.johnodonohue.com/.

O'Farrell, Pius. *Nano Nagle (1718–1774) & Francis Moylan (1735–1815)*. Cork: Cork Publishing Ltd, 2001.

———. *Nano Nagle: Woman of the Gospel*. Monasterevin, Ireland: Presentation Generalate, 1996.

O'Loughlin, Thomas. *Journeys on the Edges: The Celtic Tradition*. Traditions of Christian Spirituality. London: Darton, Longman & Todd, 2000.

O'Sullivan, Michael, and Bernadette Flanagan. *Spiritual Capital: Spirituality in Practice in Christian Perspective*. Farnham, Surrey, UK: Ashgate, 2012.

Ozelsel, Michaela M. *Forty Days: The Diary of a Traditional Solitary Sufi Retreat*. Brattleboro, VT: Threshold, 1996.

Palmer, Parker. *The Courage to Teach: Exploring the Inner Landscape of a Teacher's Life*. San Francisco: Jossey-Bass, 1998.

Panikkar, Raimundo. *Blessed Simplicity: The Monk as Universal Archetype*. New York: Seabury, 1982.

Paton, Graeme. "First-born children 'pressurised more to succeed at school.'" *The Telegraph* (London) 29 June 2009.

Patton, Kimberley Christine, and John Stratton-Hawley, editors. *Holy Tears: Weeping in the Religious Imagination*. Princeton: Princeton University Press, 2005.

Paul VI, Pope. *Ad Gentes: On the Mission Activity of the Church*. Decree proclaimed on December 7, 1965. Online: http://www.vatican.va/archive/hist_councils/ii_vatican_council/documents/vat-ii_decree_19651207_ad-gentes_en.html/.

Paulsell, Stephanie. *Honoring the Body: Meditations on a Christian Practice*. The Practices of Faith Series. San Francisco, Jossey-Bass, 2003.

Percy, Anthony. *The Theology of the Body Made Simple*. Boston: Pauline, 2006.

Peterson, Susan Carol, and Courtney Ann Vaughn-Roberson. *Women with Vision: The Presentation Sisters of South Dakota 1880–1995*. Champaign: University of Illinois Press, 1988.

Pinions. *Wind on the Sand: The Hidden Life of an Anchoress*. London: SPCK, 1980.

Plaiss, Mark, *The Inner Room: A Journey into Lay Monasticism*. Cincinnati: St. Anthony Messenger Press, 2007.

Poleman, Roger. "Une vocation d'ermite." *Vie consacrée* 48 (1976) 341–51.

Pseudo-Athanasius. *The Life & Regimen of the Blessed & Holy Teacher Syncletica*. Translated by Elizabeth Bryson Bongie. Akathist Series 3. Peregrina Translation Series 21. Toronto: Peregrina, 1996.

Rahner, Karl. *Visions and Prophecies*. Translated by Charles Henkey and Richard Strachan. Quaestiones disputatae 10. New York: Herder & Herder, 1963.

Rapley, Elizabeth. *The Dévotes: Women and Church in Seventeenth-Century France*. McGill-Queen's Studies in the History of Religion 4. Montreal: McGill-Queen's University Press, 1993.

Raughter, Rosemary. "A Discreet Benevolence: Female Philanthropy and the Catholic Resurgence in Eighteenth-Century Ireland." *Women's History Review* 6 (1997) 465–87.

Reba Place Fellowship. Online: http://www.rebaplacefellowship.org/.

Reynolds, Dana. *Ink and Honey*. Bristol, IN: Chandelles Press, 2012.

Rinpoche, Sogyal. *The Tibetan Book of Living and Dying*. San Francisco: HarperSanFrancisco, 2002.

Ritter, Beth. "Report from Sundance 2006: Religion in Independent Film." *Journal of Religion and Film* 10/1(2006). Online: http://www.unomaha.edu/jrf/vol10no1/sundance2006.htm/.

Robson, Michael J. P., editor. *The Cambridge Companion to Francis of Assisi*. Cambridge Companions to Religion. Cambridge: Cambridge University Press, 2011.

Romano, Eugene C. *A Way of Desert Spirituality: The Plan of Life of the Hermits of Bethlehem*. New York: Alba House, 1993.

Rubenson, Samuel. *The Letters of St. Antony: Monasticism and the Making of a Saint*. Minneapolis: Fortress, 1995.

Ruffing, Janet. "Encountering Love Mysticism: Issues in Supervision." *Presence* 1 (January 1995) 20–33.

———. *To Tell the Sacred Tale: Spiritual Direction and Narrative*. New York: Paulist, 2011.

Russell, Bertrand. *Conquest of Happiness*. New York: Liveright, 1930.

Sacred Life Arts. Online: http://sacredlifearts.com/.

Sardello, Robert. *Silence*. Benson, NC: Goldstone, 2006.

Savage, Anne, and Nicholas Watson, translators. *Anchoritic Spirituality: "Ancrene Wisse" and Associated Works*. The Classics of Western Spirituality. New York: Paulist, 1991.

Schaffer, Mary. *The Life and Regimen of the Blessed and Holy Syncletica: Part Two: A Study of the Life*. Eugene, OR: Wipf & Stock, 2005.

Schelling, F. W. J. *Samtliche Werke*. Edited by K. F. A. Schelling. 14 vols. Stuttgart: Cotta, 1856–1861.

Schneiders, Sandra. *Finding the Treasure: Locating Catholic Religious Life in a New Ecclesial and Cultural Context*. 'Religious Life in the New Millennium, Vol. 1. Mahwah, NJ: Paulist, 2000.

———. *The Revelatory Text: Interpreting the New Testament as Sacred Scripture*. Collegeville, MN: Liturgical, 1999

———. *Selling All: Commitment, Consecrated Celibacy, and Community in Catholic Religious Life*. Religious Life in the New Millennium 2. Mahwah, NJ: Paulist, 2001.

Schüssler Fiorenza, Elisabeth. *Bread Not Stone: The Challenge of Feminist Biblical Interpretation*. 10th anniversary edition. Boston: Beacon, 1995

Seelaus, Vilma, "Traditions of Spiritual Guidance: The Self—Mirror of God." *The Way* 32/3 (1992) n.p.

Sharma, Robert S. *The Monk Who Sold His Ferrari: A Fable about Fulfilling Your Dreams and Reaching Your Destiny*. San Francisco: HarperSanFrancisco, 1997.

Sharpe, Richard. *Medieval Irish Saints' Lives: An Introduction to Vitae Sanctorum Hiberniae*. Oxford: Clarendon, 1991.

Sheldrake, Philip. "Revising Historical Perspectives." *The Way Supplement* 65 (1989) 66–77

Shute, Michael. *Boudica the Great: An Epic Narrative Biographical Poem*. London: Archangel, 2011.

Simons, Walter. *Cities of Ladies: Beguine Communities in the Medieval Low Countries 1200–1565*. The Middle Ages Series. Philadelphia: University of Pennsylvania Press, 2003.

The Simple Way. Online: http://www.thesimpleway.org/

Simpson, Ray. *High Street Monasteries: Fresh Expression of Committed Christianity*. Stowmarket, Sussex: Kevin Mayhew, 2009.

Sinetar, Marsha. *Ordinary People as Monks & Mystics: Lifestyles for Spiritual Wholeness* Rev. ed. New York: Paulist, 2007.

Sizoo, Lysanne. "Kumla Prison Monastery: Taking the Next Step." *The Way* 49/1 (2010) 93–104.

———. "When Cell Doors Close and Hearts Open." *The Way* 43/4 (2004) 161–68.

Soelle, Dorothee. *The Silent Cry: Mysticism and Resistance.* Minneapolis: Fortress, 2001.

Spink, Peter, editor. *The Universal Christ: Daily Readings with Bede Griffiths.* Modern Spirituality Series. London: Darton, Longman & Todd, 1993.

Stevenot-Sullivan, Susan. "How Can This Be?: The New Mystery of Monastic Vocation." *Benedictines* (1999) 26–31.

Stone, Mary Ignatius, OSU. *Commentary on the Writings of Saint Angela Merici: Rule, Counsels, Legacies.* England: Unpublished, 1996.

Swan, Laura, *The Forgotten Desert Mothers: Sayings, Lives, and Stories of Early Christian Women.* New York: Paulist, 2001.

Swimme, Brian, and Thomas Berry. *The Universe Story from the Primordial Flaring Forth to the Ecozoic Era: A Celebration of the Unfolding of the Cosmos.* San Francisco: HarperSanFrancisco, 1992

Sylvester, Nancy, and Mary Jo Klick. *Crucible for Change: Engaging Impasse through Communal Contemplation and Dialogue.* San Antonio: Sor Juana, 2004.

Tacey, David. *The Spirituality Revolution: The Emergence of Contemporary Spirituality.* Sydney: HarperCollins, 2003; London: Brunner-Routledge, 2004.

Talbot, John Michael. *The Universal Monk: The Way of the New Monastics.* Collegeville, MN: Liturgical, 2011.

———. *The World Is My Cloister: Living from the Hermit Within.* Maryknoll, NY: Orbis, 2010.

Taylor, Barbara Erakko. *Silence: Making the Journey to Inner Quiet.* Philadelphia: Inisfree, 1997.

———. *Silent Dwellers: Embracing the Solitary Life.* New York: Continuum, 1999.

Taylor, Charles. *A Secular Age.* Cambridge, UK: Belknap, 2007.

Teasdale, Wayne. *A Monk in the World: Cultivating a Spiritual Life.* Novato, CA: New World Library, 2002.

———. *The Mystic Heart: Discovering a Universal Spirituality in the World's Religions.* Novato, CA: New World Library, 1999.

Teilhard de Chardin, Pierre. *The Divine Milieu: An Essay on the Interior Life.* Translated by Bernard Wall. London: Fontana, 1978

Tenzin Palmo, Jetsunma. *Into the Heart of Life.* Ithaca, NY: Snow Lion, 2011.

———. *Reflections on a Mountain Lake: Teachings on Practical Buddhism.* Ithaca, NY: Snow Lion, 2002.

———. *Three Teachings: A Compilation of Talks Given in Singapore, in 1998.* Singapore: KMSPKS Monastery, 2000.

Teresa, of Avila, Saint. *The Collected Works of St. Teresa of Avila.* 3 vols. Translated by Kieran Kavanaugh, OCD, and Otilio Rodriguez, OCD. Washington DC: ICS, 1980

Thiers, Jean Baptiste. *Traité de la clôture des religieuses.* Paris: Dezallier, 1681.

Thomas, Charles. "Rosnat, Rostat, and the Early Irish Church", *Ériu* 22(1971) 100–106.

Tiso, Francis V. "Raimundo Panikkar on the Monk as Archetype." *Monastic Interreligious Dialogue* 1/2 (July–December 2011). Online: http://www.dimmid.org/index. asp?Type=B_BASIC&SEC={383FB138-0B7E-4BB4-9629-665574E6B40C/.

Tolle, Eckhart. *The Power of Now: A Guide to Spiritual Enlightenment*. London: Hodder & Stoughton, 2005.

Tomaine, Jane. *St. Benedict's Toolbox: The Nuts and Bolts of Everyday Benedictine Living* Harrisburg, PA: Morehouse, 2005.

Trungpa, Chögyam. *The Myth of Freedom and the Way of Meditation*. Boston: Shambhala, 2005.

Turner, Victor, and Edith Turner. *Image and Pilgrimage in Christian Culture: Anthropological Perspectives*. Lectures on the History of Religions 11. New York: Colombia University Press, 1995.

Underhill, Evelyn. *Mysticism: A Study in the Nature and Development of Man's Spiritual Consciousness*. London: Methuen, 1930.

Verter, Bradford. "Spiritual Capital: Theorizing Religion with Bourdieu against Bourdieu." *Sociological Theory* 21 (2003) 150–74.

Vest, Norvene, *Desiring Life: Benedict on Wisdom and the Good Life*. Cambridge: Cowley, 2000.

———. *Friend of the Soul: A Benedictine Spirituality of Work*. Cambridge: Cowley, 1997.

———. *No Moment Too Small: Rhythms of Silence, Prayer, and Holy Reading*. Kalamazoo: Cistercian, 1994.

Viola, Frank. *From Eternity to Here: Rediscovering the Ageless Purpose of God*. Colorado Springs: David C. Cook, 2009.

Waaijman, Kees. *Spirituality: Forms, Foundations, Methods*. Studies in Spirituality Supplment 8. Leuven: Peeters, 2002.

Walters, John. *Mind Unshaken: A Modern Approach to Buddhism*. London: Rider, 1971.

Walsh, Timothy John. *Nano and the Presentation Sisters*. Monasterevin, Ireland: Presentation Gerneralate, 1980.

Ward, Benedicta, translator. *The Sayings of the Desert Fathers: The Alphabetical Collection*. Kalamazoo: Cistercian, 1975

Warren, Frederick Edward, editor. *The Antiphonary of Bangor: An Early Irish Manuscript in the Ambrosian Library at Milan, 1895*. Whitefish, MT: Kessinger, 2010.

Weaver, Judith. "An American Desert Mother." *Raven's Bread* 2/3 (1998) 3–4.

Webster, Helen Noyes. *Herbs: How to Grow Them and How to Use Them*. Rev. ed. Boston: Branford, 1947.

Weil, Simone. *Waiting for God*. Translated by Emma Craufurd. Perennial Classics. New York: Perennial, 2001.

Wheatley, Margaret J., and Myron Kellner-Rogers. *A Simpler Way*. San Francisco: Berrett-Koehler, 1996.

Wheeler, Bonnie, editor. *Listening to Heloise: The Voice of a Twelfth-Century Woman*. The New Middle Ages. New York: St. Martin's, 1999.

Whelan, Michael, editor. *Issues for Church and Society in Australia: The Aquinas Jubilee Lectures* Sydney: St Pauls, 2006.

Wilson, Jonathan R. *Living Faithfully in a Fragmented World: Lessons from MacIntyre's "After Virtue."* Harrisburg, PA: Trinity, 1995.

Wilson-Hartgrove, Jonathan. *To Baghdad and Beyond: How I Got Born Again in Babylon*. Eugene, OR: Cascade Books, 2005.

Wimbush, Vincent L., editor. *Ascetic Behavior in Greco-Roman Antiquity: A Sourcebook*. Studies in Antiquity & Christianity. Minneapolis: Fortress, 1990.

Wolfteich, Claire. "Standing at the Gap: Reading Classics and the Practices of Everyday Life." *Spiritus: A Journal of Christian Spirituality* 10/2 (2010) 251–56.

Wolski-Conn, Joann, editor. *Women's Spirituality: Resources for Christian Development.* 2nd ed. New York: Paulist, 1996.

Worthen, Molly, "The Unexpected Monks." *The Boston Globe*, February 3, 2008. Online: http://prayerfoundation.org/dailyoffice/y_boston_globe_the_unexpected_monks.htm/.

Zemon-Davis, Natalie, and Arlette Farge, editors. *A History of Women in the West.* Vol. 3, *Renaissance and Enlightenment Paradoxes.* Cambridge: Harvard University Press, 1995.

Made in the USA
Middletown, DE
18 March 2018